MW00635997

Pastor G Library
990 NE 125th Street, Suite 200
North Miami, FL 33161
Website: www.tabernacleofglory.net
Email: pastorgslibrary@gmail.com
(305) 899-0101

ISBN : 978-1-63949-000-4

To my wife, Patricia,
my companion in life,
and
my blessed sons
Gregory, Jr., and Joshua

The Royal Family
Volume 2

How to live as a son of the Kingdom

"You have made them members of a royal family. You have made them priests to serve our God. They will rule on the earth."
(Revelation 5:10, NIRV)

by
Gregory Toussaint

Table of Contents

How to live as a son of the Kingdom

"Sonship is a process. Like physical growth, spiritual growth happens gradually. Many people forfeit the blessings of their sonship because they lose heart along the way"

Gregory Toussaint

April 1ˢᵗ

Sonship is a Status

KEY VERSE

"The field is the world, the good seeds are the sons of the king-dom, but the tares are the sons of the wicked one"
(Matthew 13:38, NKJV)

God's kingdom functions like a family. It has fathers, moth-ers, and sons. So far, we have seen the responsibilities of the parents. Now, we are going to look at the role of sons.

We must first establish that sonship is a status. For exam-ple, when a child is born in the United States, so long as he is under 18, he is considered a minor. As such, without the consent of an adult, most of the privileges given to citizens of the country are inaccessible to him. He cannot obtain a driver's license, get married, rent a house, get a credit card, etc. However, when that child turns 18, the law declares him an adult. Suddenly, all of the privileges that were out of reach for him before now become accessible because his status has changed. When you become a son, your spiritual status in heaven is changed from minor to adult. At that mo-ment, the blessings of the kingdom become available to you. This is what the apostle Paul meant when he said, *"The heir as long as he is a child is no different from a slave, though he is <u>owner of everything</u>"* (Galatians 4:1). May the Lord help us grow so our spiritual status can change.

Prayer

Father God, I desire to have the heart of a son. In Jesus' name, I pray. Amen

Application

What are some spiritual habits will you need to cultivate today as you seek to claim your inheritance as son or daughter in the kingdom?

Hearing the voice of God

_____

_____

_____

_____

_____

_____

_____

_____

_____

_____

Bible in a year
1 Samuel 21 – 1 Samuel 23

April 2

Sonship is a Mentality

KEY VERSE

"The field is the world, the good seeds are the sons of the kingdom, but the tares are the sons of the wicked one"
(Matthew 13:38, NKJV)

Sonship is not only a status but also a mentality. Paul, before his death, said, *"I have fought the good fight, I have <u>finished</u> the race, I have kept the faith. Now there is in store for me the crown of righteousness"* (2 Timothy 4:7-8). The Apostle is saying here that he was able to walk into his inheritance, which is the prerogative of a son (Gal. 4:7). Before becoming a spiritual adult, a son, he was a child. He described his spiritual childhood saying, *"When I was a child, I <u>spoke</u> as a child, I <u>understood</u> as a child, I thought as a child; but when I became a man, I put away childish <u>things</u>"* (1 Corinthians 13:11 NKJV). Notice that childhood and adulthood have to do with the way you "think," the way you "understand" things, the way you "speak," and the things you do. Thus, spiritual childishness is a mentality that affects both your thoughts and actions. Ask God to renew your mind with the Word today so you can walk like a son (Romans 12:1-2).

Prayer

Lord, renew my mind with your Word today. Let my thoughts and actions be evident to a son. Amen

Application

Identify any childhood behavior(s) that work against your desire to attain sonship in Christ. What changes are you trusting God would take place this week?

Hearing the voice of God

_____

_____

_____

_____

_____

_____

_____

_____

_____

_____

Bible in a year
1 Samuel 24 – 1 Samuel 26

April 3

Sonship is an Attitude

KEY VERSE

"The field is the world, the good seeds are the sons of the kingdom, but the tares are the sons of the wicked one"
(Matthew 13:38, NKJV)

Sonship is not only a status and mentality, but also an attitude. We had previously mentioned that being a "son" means being a "spiritual adult." But what characterizes spiritual adulthood? It is an attitude governed by love. Paul says, *"Love suffers long and is kind; love does not envy; love does not parade itself, is not puffed up; does not behave rudely, does not seek its own, is not provoked, thinks no evil; does not rejoice in iniquity but rejoices in the truth; bears all things, believes all things, hopes all things, endures all things. Love never fails..."* (1 Corinthians 13:4-8, NKJV). All these characteristics of love are connected with attitude. Then Paul concludes, *"When I was a child, I spoke as a child, I understood as a child, I thought as a child; but when I became a man, I put away childish things"* (1 Corinthians 13:11, NKJV). A child's attitude is governed by fear, anger, pride, and bitterness, but a son's attitude is governed by love. If you want to know whether you have grown from being a child to being a son, check to see if you possess the characteristics described in 1 Corinthians 13 verses 4-8. Are they present in your everyday life?

Prayer

Holy Spirit of God, fill my heart with love so I may be a witness to Your Word. In Jesus' name, I pray. Amen

Application

Which of these negative characteristics given above do you think people in your circle would use to describe you, and what are you doing today to change that image?

Hearing the voice of God

_____
_____
_____
_____
_____
_____
_____
_____
_____
_____
_____

Bible in a year
1 Samuel 27 – 1 Samuel 31

April 4

Sonship is a Process

KEY VERSE

"The field is the world, the good seeds are the sons of the kingdom, but the tares are the sons of the wicked one"

(Matthew 13:38, NKJV)

Jesus was promised to be called the Son of God the day he was conceived. The Angel said to Mary, *"He will be great and will be called the Son of the Highest, and the Lord God will give Him the throne of His father, David"* (Luke 1:32, NKJV). However, his full sonship was not realized until He ascended to the right hand of the father, who said to Him, *"You are My Son, Today I have begotten You"* (Hebrews 1:5, NKJV). It took 30 years for His sonship to develop fully. Sonship is a process. Like physical growth, spiritual growth occurs gradually. Many people forfeit the blessings of their sonship, because they lose heart along the way. Ask God to strengthen you.

Prayer

Jesus my Lord, I pray for a heart like yours in order to withstand the challenges that come with the process. In Your name, I pray. Amen

Application

In what area do you feel you need to grow more spiritually, and what will you do today to begin that beautiful journey?

Hearing the voice of God

_____

_____

_____

_____

_____

_____

_____

_____

_____

_____

Bible in a year
2 Samuel 1 – 2 Samuel 3

April 5

Sonship: The connection stage

KEY VERSE

"The field is the world, the good seeds are the sons of the king-dom, but the tares are the sons of the wicked one"
(Matthew 13:38, NKJV)

Sonship is a process that comprises many stages. During His 30 years of development, Jesus went through many stages, which we will go through as well. Let us see them.

First, there is the connection stage. At this stage, a son becomes aware of a father's role in his life and is connected with him. Jesus went through that stage at an early age. One time Jesus went to Jerusalem with his parents. When the festivities were over, the parents took the road back to return home. Along the way, they realized that Jesus was missing. So, they went back to the temple to find Him. They said to Him, *"your father has been looking for you anxiously,"* but He answered, *"Why did you seek Me? Did you not know that I must be about My Father's business?"* (Luke 2:49, NKJV). Jesus became aware of his spiritual sonship and was so connected to His Father's presence that He did not want to leave the temple. The first step to becoming a son is to be spiritually connected with a father, like Jesus to his Heavenly Father (John 10:30) and Elisha to spiritual father (1 Kings 19:21). Nothing can happen in the father-son relationship until that connection occurs in your heart (Mal. 4:6). Unfortunately, many believers fight at this stage and never progress in their sonship. They are afraid of letting go of who they are to become and who they should be. Are you willing to be connected with a spiritual father? Have you accepted his role in your life?

Prayer

Father God, I command fear, pride, anger, and bitterness to lose me so I may let go of who I am to become who you have called me to be. In Jesus' name, I pray. Amen

Application

What personal sacrifice are you committing to making today and onward as you progress into sonship status?

Hearing the voice of God

_____

_____

_____

_____

_____

_____

_____

_____

_____

_____

_____

Bible in a year
2 Samuel 4–2 Samuel 7

April 6

Sonship: The Training Stage

KEY VERSE

"The field is the world, the good seeds are the sons of the kingdom, but the tares are the sons of the wicked one"
(Matthew 13:38, NKJV)

Once the spiritual connection occurs in the heart of the son, the next stage is training. Training begins when he makes himself available to serve. The purpose of serving is to develop positive character traits such as love, faithfulness, humility, etc. This aspect of training is done through delegation of menial tasks. For example, David kept his father's sheep (1 Sam. 17:34). Elisha poured water for Elijah (2 Kings 3:11). Joshua ran errands for Moses (Num. 11:28).

Jesus had to go through the training stage as well. Even though for most of His life He had the noble mission of preaching the Gospel, healing the sick, raising the dead, and eventually saving humanity, for many years, He simply did the work of a carpenter. This is why when He began in ministry, they said, *"Is this not the carpenter, the Son of Mary, and brother of James, Joses, Judas, and Simon? And are not His sisters here with us?"* (Mark 6:3, NKJV). During those years of obscurity, He was developing character. The Bible states, *"And the Child grew and became strong in spirit, filled with wisdom; and the grace of God was upon Him."* (Luke 2:40, NKJV). Imagine how painful the thirtieth birthday of Jesus must have been. He knew that He had thirty-three years to live. He was now turning thirty, which means about 90% of His life on earth was gone. But He was not doing "ministry;" He was simply cutting wood. He had to trust that His Father in heaven knew what He was doing. Many sons try to shorten the training stage. But in reality they make it longer. Like the children of Israel, they change an eleven-day journey into 40 years. Trust the process.

Prayer

Father God, help me to keep my eyes focused on you and not the numbers. In Jesus' name, I pray. Amen

Application

What do you plan to do so that you may develop patience while following the Father's plan? Take the time to write those things down.

Hearing the voice of God

_____
_____
_____
_____
_____
_____
_____
_____
_____
_____

Bible in a year
2 Samuel 8–2 Samuel 11

April 7

Sonship: The Maturing Stage

KEY VERSE

"The field is the world, the good seeds are the sons of the kingdom, but the tares are the sons of the wicked one"
(Matthew 13:38, NKJV)

The third stage is the maturing stage. At this stage, a father administers different tests to a son to determine both strength and weakness. As a Son, Jesus went through the maturing stage also. He waited for the Father's directives for thirty years. At the age of thirty, God sent John the Baptist as a voice in the wilderness to prepare His way. When He began His ministry, Jesus came to be baptized. At that moment, a voice came out of heaven saying, *"This is my son in whom I am well-pleased"* (Matthew 3:17). Immediately after, the Bible states, *"Jesus was led by the Spirit out into the desert to be put to the test by the devil"* (Matthew 4:1, NJB). As soon as Jesus reached the maturing stage, He was tested. Paul, as a spiritual father, also tested his son Timothy. In writing to Christians of Philippi, he said of him, *"But you know his proven character, that as a son with his father he served with me in the gospel"* (Philippians 2:22, NKJV). Paul had tested Timothy's character and testified that Timothy had succeeded. A father likewise evaluates character to determine strengths and weaknesses. He will require his son to grow in certain areas in his life and will challenge him to face his weaknesses. A son will not be perfect but must show improvements. How do you react when challenged to grow in certain areas? Do you get defensive?-

Or do you take feedback graciously and do your best to grow?

Prayer

Lord, grant me a humble spirit to graciously receive feedback and a discerning heart to pass the test. In Your Holy name, I pray. Amen.

Application

What character trait do you have a determination to see improvement in, and what steps will you be taking in that direction today?

Hearing the voice of God

_____

_____

_____

_____

_____

_____

_____

_____

_____

_____

Bible in a year
2 Samuel 12 – 2 Samuel 14

April 8

Sonship: The Promotion Stage

KEY VERSE

"The field is the world, the good seeds are the sons of the kingdom, but the tares are the sons of the wicked one"

(Matthew 13:38, NKJV)

When the son has grown in character and has proven himself, he is given a new level of responsibility. This is the promotion stage. After Jesus had served as a carpenter in the shadows for many years and had been tested in the wilderness, the Bible says, *"Jesus went about all Galilee, <u>teaching</u> in their synagogues, preaching the gospel of the kingdom, and <u>healing</u> all kinds of sickness and all kinds of disease among the people. Then <u>His fame</u> went throughout all Syria…"* (Matthew 4:23–24, NKJV). God, the Father, did not release Jesus in public until He had been fully processed in the shadows. During the stage of promotion, a son will grow in visibility, popularity, and influence. Thus, the text states, *"His fame went throughout Syria."* And at that stage, a son must be taught how to handle God's promotion and rewards at this stage.

Prayer

Lord, fill me with Your seven spirits in order to be effective in the handling of Your mysteries. In Your name, Christ I pray. Amen.

Application

How are you planning to be more effective and faithful with your current responsibilities while in the shadows as you wait patiently for the Lord to manifest His glory through you?

Hearing the voice of God

_____

_____

_____

_____

_____

_____

_____

_____

_____

_____

Bible in a year
2 Samuel 15 – 2 Samuel 17

April 9

Sonship: The Inheritance Stage

<u>KEY VERSE</u>

"The field is the world, the good seeds are the sons of the king-dom, but the tares are the sons of the wicked one"
(Matthew 13:38, NKJV)

The last stage in the sonship process is inheritance. The Bible says, *"Therefore you are no longer a slave but a son, and if a son, then an heir of God through Christ"* (Galatians 4:7, NKJV). A son is an heir. He begins to walk in certain aspects of his destiny when he reaches this stage. Notice the word "begin"; you do not receive in God all at once. The Lord said to Israel when he was going to drive the Canaanites out of the land, *"Little by little I will drive them out from before you until you have increased, and you inherit the land"* (Exodus 23:30, NKJV). God did not give the Israelites their inheritance all at once. He did it little by little. Why? The Lord explains, *"I will not drive them out from before you in one year, lest the land becomes desolate and the beasts of the field become too numerous for you"* (Exodus 23:29, NKJV). In other words, if He gives them their inheritance all at once it will be too much for them to manage. Further-more, wild animals will take advantage of them. A blessing received before time becomes a curse. Ask God to give you the patience to wait on Him.

Prayer

Lord God, You have established my inheritance since the foundation of the world. To possess it, I seek Your patience today. Amen.

Application

In what area(s) will you need to practice patience today while trusting and waiting on the Lord to grant you your spiritual inheritance?

Hearing the voice of God

_____
_____
_____
_____
_____
_____
_____
_____
_____
_____

Bible in a year
2 Samuel 18 – 2 Samuel 19

April 10

The Inheritance Comes in Many Installments

KEY VERSE

*"The field is the world, the good seeds are the sons of the king-
dom, but the tares are the sons of the wicked one"*
(Matthew 13:38, NKJV)

Since God gives us our blessing in portions, our inheritance
also comprises different installments. At each stage of sonship, you receive a greater part of your inheritance. Jesus
was declared Son three times. In each instance, He received
a new level of grace. He was declared Son of God for the
first time at His baptism. While He stood in the Jordan river,
a voice came out of heaven and said, *"This is My beloved Son,
in whom I am well pleased"* (Matthew 3:17, NKJV). At that time,
Jesus received the first installment of his inheritance. He was
given the power to preach, teach, and work miracles (Matt.
4:23-24).

Jesus was declared Son a second time at His resurrection. The Bibles states, *"...Jesus Christ our Lord, who was born
of the seed of David according to the flesh, and <u>declared</u> to be the
<u>Son of God</u> with power according to the Spirit of holiness, by the
resurrection from the dead"* (Romans 1:3–4, NKJV). The resurrection from the dead was a declaration of Christ's sonship. At that time, He received the second installment of
His inheritance, which was a glorified body. He was given a
body that was flesh enough to eat food (Luke 24:42-43) and
the spirit enough to go through a wall (John 20:19, NKJV).

He was declared Son of God for the third time, 40 days after his resurrection, when he ascended to heaven. The author of Hebrews states,

God, who at various times and in various ways spoke in time past to the fathers by the prophets, has in these last days spoken to us by His Son… when He had by Himself purged our sins, sat down at the right hand of the Majesty on high, …as He has by inheritance obtained a more excellent name than they. For to which of the angels did He ever say: "You are My Son, Today I have begotten You"? (Hebrews 1:1-5).

When Jesus Christ was declared Son the third time, he received the third part of his inheritance. The Father granted Him the most important seat in the kingdom, after His own. He made him sit at "the right hand of Majesty on high," where He rules over His enemies.

In short, there are many stages of sonship. You should not be satisfied with the level of sonship that you have now; you should trust God for the next level. Ask the Lord to show you how you can grow in your sonship.

Prayer

Father God, I pray for the aptitude of Your beloved Son in order to receive all of the installments of my inheritance. In His precious name, I pray. Amen.

Application

What stage of inheritance do you believe you are now operating in, and what will you begin to do today in order to access a higher level of inheritance?

Hearing the voice of God

_____

_____

_____

_____

_____

_____

_____

_____

_____

_____

Bible in a year
2 Samuel 20 – 2 Samuel 22

April 11
The Father Determines the Process

KEY VERSE

"The field is the world, the good seeds are the sons of the kingdom, but the tares are the sons of the wicked one"
(Matthew 13:38, NKJV)

The Heavenly Father determined the duration of each sonship stage in Jesus' life. It is the Heavenly Father, through a spiritual father, who determines the season in a son's life, not the son himself. The Bible says, *"Now I say that the <u>heir</u>, as long as he is a child, does not differ at all from a slave, though he is master of all, but is under guardians and stewards until the time <u>appointed by the father.</u>"* (Galatians 4:1-2). Notice, until the time appointed by the father! I have often been in a position to challenge sons who have not grown spiritually; they would often retort, "Oh no, I have grown a lot spiritually over the years." They often ignore that "maturity" is not a feeling in your heart. It is a change that begins in your heart that leads to modified behavior. Therefore, everyone notices when you are maturing spiritually, especially those in authority over your life. True sons learn to trust the judgment of those who are ahead, particularly spiritual parents.

Some people get discouraged in the sonship journey because they expect to walk into their inheritance as sons immediately. As a result, they forfeit their birthright for privileges of lesser value. As a son, you must learn to cultivate patience.

Prayer

Father God, as a son, I totally surrender the process into Your mighty hands. In the name of Jesus Christ the Lord, I pray. Amen.

Application

How do you plan to avoid the inevitable traps, deceptions, and temptations of the enemy that would entice you to take a shortcut from the process or to avoid it altogether?

Hearing the voice of God

_____

_____

_____

_____

_____

_____

_____

_____

_____

_____

Bible in a year
2 Samuel 23 – 2 Samuel 24

April 12

The Privilege of a Son

KEY VERSE
"The field is the world, the good seeds are the sons of the kingdom, but the tares are the sons of the wicked one"
(Matthew 13:38, NKJV)

Being a son is a great privilege. Alluding to Jesus, the book of Hebrews says, *"To which of the angels did He [God] ever say: "You are My son, today I have begotten you"* (Hebrews 1:5, NKJV). The author presents the angels as servants and Jesus as His Son. Therefore, He is highly superior to them.

One time, while I was teaching sonship, one of my students told me how he lost a job for ignoring this truth. He told me he was working in New York for a Jew. This man made him the general manager in his factory. The boss's son was working under him. The son was in one of the lowest positions at the company. Every time the son made a mistake; the father severely admonished him. The son was treated more severely than all of the other employees. Seeing the father scolding his son this way, the general manager thought he could do the same. One day the son had a mishap, and the employee reprimanded him severely as the father would do. The owner of the company called the manager and fired him. He reminded the manager that the young man that he was yelling at was his son: the heir of the company! That day, he understood the difference between a servant and a son. Thank God in the kingdom, even though we all serve, we are sons. You are special. You are a son of the kingdom.

Prayer

Father God, I rejoice today in knowing that I am a son of the kingdom. Amen.

Application

How does the privilege of sonship inspire you to become the best version of yourself today?

Hearing the voice of God

_____

_____

_____

_____

_____

_____

_____

_____

_____

_____

Bible in a year
1 King 1 – 1 King 2

April 13

A Son Knows Who He Is

KEY VERSE

"The field is the world, the good seeds are the sons of the kingdom, but the tares are the sons of the wicked one"

(Matthew 13:38, NKJV)

The most significant difference between a son and a slave is that the slave doesn't know who he is, but a son does. During colonial times, slaves were bought as a commodity. The slave was considered a property. The master would say about the slave, "This is mine, don't touch it." Treating a person like a thing is the greatest evil behind slavery. It deals a fatal blow to a person's sense of dignity. The slave struggles with his sense of identity. He is not sure whether he is a man or a thing. A person with a slave mentality struggles with self-esteem. When a Christian doesn't know who he is, he thinks like a slave. But, the Bible says, *"You are no longer a slave, but a son, if a son, then a heir of God through Christ"* (Galatians 2:20, NKJV). Everything revolves around identity. The prodigal son was living a miserable life, but the day he remembered who he was, his life changed for the better. So, how do you see yourself? The day you genuinely see yourself like a son, everything will change..

Prayer

Heavenly Father, I thank you for giving me a spiritual father. I am a son in a royal family. Amen.

Application

In what area of your life today will you begin to apply sonship behaviors, and what will these changes look like?

Hearing the voice of God

_____

_____

_____

_____

_____

_____

_____

_____

_____

Bible in a year
1 King 3 – 1 King 5

April 14

A Son Has a Sense of Dignity

KEY VERSE

*"The field is the world, the good seeds are the sons of the king-
dom, but the tares are the sons of the wicked one"*
(Matthew 13:38, NKJV)

Everyone is born with a sense of dignity. A homeless
person may be sleeping under a bridge, but he will react if
you cross him the wrong way. He carries a natural sense of
dignity that his life circumstances do not change. Where
does that sense of dignity come from? It comes from the
following words, *"Let Us make man in Our image, according to
our likes"* (Genesis 1:26, NKJV). Man carries the image of
God and, therefore, has a natural sense of dignity. Being a
son means. "I am not a fluke of nature." "I have a spiritual
origin." "I have a Heavenly Father and a spiritual father." "
I am not an orphan." "I am not left in a desert by myself."
"I have spiritual parents." If you are a son in the house, you
should also be proud of that fact..

Prayer

God of Creation, thank You for giving me an identity in You since the creation of man. In the name of Jesus Christ, I pray. Amen.

Application

How does the definition of sonship explained in today's lesson influence your view on the concept? Do you see yourself as someone with a sonship mentality or are you still developing it?

Hearing the voice of God

_____

_____

_____

_____

_____

_____

_____

_____

_____

_____

_____

Bible in a year
1 King 6 – 1 King 7

The Problem of Slavery

KEY VERSE

"The field is the world, the good seeds are the sons of the kingdom, but the tares are the sons of the wicked one"
(Matthew 13:38, NKJV)

The Bible establishes a clear difference between spiritual slaves and sons. It says, *"You are no longer a <u>slave</u>, but a <u>son</u>"* (Colossians 2:20, NKJV). One of the best ways to understand spiritual slavery is to first look at it in the natural (1 Cor. 15:46). Slavery crushes a man's sense of dignity. When a person becomes a slave, he is treated as property. Slaves were bought, sold, leased, rented out, and gifted. Slaves were treated as properties, and as a result, they saw themselves as such. Properties are not loved, they are used.

It is not difficult to identify people who operate with a slave mentality in the kingdom. While everyone else is working just as hard as them and is doing so joyfully, they, on the other hand, feel like they are being exploited. A slave thinks like this because he sees himself as property. A son does not. A son sees himself as someone serving in his own house and is happy to do so. Which mentality do you have? That of a slave or a son?

Prayer

Father God, I rebuke all mentalities that are those of a slave. I embrace the identity and mentality of a son. In the Lord's name, I pray Amen.

Application

How will you begin to transform the mentality of a slave to one of a son? How will this new perspective differ?

Hearing the voice of God

_____

_____

_____

_____

_____

_____

_____

_____

_____

_____

_____

Bible in a year
1 King 8

April 16

A Slave Mentality Creates Fear

KEY VERSE
"The field is the world, the good seeds are the sons of the king-dom, but the tares are the sons of the wicked one"
(Matthew 13:38, NKJV)

The emotion that dominates the life of a slave is fear. But the one that dominates the life of a son is love. A slave performs because he is afraid of being chastised. A son performs because he knows he is loved and wants love in return. Hence, the Bible says, *"For you did not receive the spirit of bondage again to fear, but you received the Spirit of adoption by whom we cry out, "Abba, Father."* (Romans 8:15,NKJV). What is your ground motive for serving God? You should not serve because you are afraid of going to hell. You should serve Him because you are grateful for heaven.

Prayer

My God, You have not given me a spirit of fear, but rather a spirit of power and a sound mind. I receive a sound mind today in Jesus' name. Amen.

Application

How can you begin to use the spirit of love within you today to cast away all emotions of fear out of your life?

Hearing the voice of God

_____

_____

_____

_____

_____

_____

_____

_____

_____

_____

_____

Bible in a year
1 King 9 – 1 King 11

April 17

A Slave Mentality Creates Pride

KEY VERSE

"The field is the world, the good seeds are the sons of the kingdom, but the tares are the sons of the wicked one"
(Matthew 13:38, NKJV)

Slavery, as we said, crushes a man's sense of dignity and leads to low self-esteem. A person in that frame of mind sees himself as inferior to others and, therefore, feels the need to elevate himself. Hence, pride is the other face of low self-esteem. When you see a person who keeps bragging about who he is and what he knows or owns, know that you are dealing with someone with a slave mentality. He feels the need to elevate himself because he feels low.

Slaves have a hard time humbling themselves, but sons have no problem doing so. The Son of God poured water in a basin and knelt to wash His disciples' feet. We read the following words, *"Jesus knowing that the <u>Father</u> had given <u>all things</u> into His hands and that He came <u>from God</u> and was going <u>to God</u>, rose from supper and laid aside His garments, took a towel and girded himself"* (John 13:3, NKJV). Jesus was able to humble Himself because He was sure of His identity as the Son and Heir of God. Do you feel demeaned when you have to fold chairs, mop the floor, or clean the bathroom? Are you the kind of person who feels like you have to do something on stage or in the spotlight to be important? That's pride! That's a slave mentality. You need to crucify it.

Prayer

In the mighty name of Jesus, I make this declaration: I rebuke and revoke a slave mentality. I am a son. Amen.

Application

Seek an opportunity today to do something humbling for someone without expecting anything in return, for example, carwash, grocery shopping, house cleaning, etc., or look for an opportunity to congratulate someone.

Hearing the voice of God

_____

_____

_____

_____

_____

_____

_____

_____

_____

_____

Bible in a year
1 King 12 – 1 King 13

April 18
A Slave Mentality Creates Vanity

KEY VERSE
"The field is the world, the good seeds are the sons of the kingdom, but the tares are the sons of the wicked one"
(Matthew 13:38, NKJV)

People with a slave mentality tend to be vain. They like to show off. Since they do not feel valuable, they think that others do not view them as valuable either. They compensate for that by putting on an act. Jesus, as a Son, did not feel the need to flaunt his abilities. In fact, He was so simple that when He silenced the winds on the sea of Galilee, the disciples said, *"What kind of man is this? Even the winds and the waves obey Him"* (Matt. 8:27, NKJV). Do you feel the need to be flashy? Are you the kind of person who is always fighting for the front seat so you can be seen? Do you feel worthless if you sit in an unseen area in the crowd? Ask God to deliver you. It is a slave mentality. You are not a slave. You are a son. Be humble.

Prayer
Father God, may the mentality of Your Son, my savior, Jesus Christ fill my heart today. In His precious name, I pray. Amen.

Application

Because you are a beloved son in the kingdom of God, look for opportunities to value others today either through words or action.

Hearing the voice of God

_____

_____

_____

_____

_____

_____

_____

_____

_____

_____

Bible in a year
1 King 14 – 1 King 16

April 19
A Slave Mentality Creates Wastefulness

KEY VERSE

"The field is the world, the good seeds are the sons of the kingdom, but the tares are the sons of the wicked one"
(Matthew 13:38, NKJV)

People who have a slave mentality tend to be wasteful. When they have an unexpected sum, instead of saving, they go out and blow it. For someone with a slave mentality, even when you give him one million dollars, he will be penniless in six months. His extravagance of living and buying useless things will cause his bankruptcy. This person would think that he could build his self-esteem by buying expensive accessories. He will not hesitate to buy a pair of glasses for an extra sum just to come to church. Don't get me wrong; it is not a problem to buy glasses for that price if you need them. But if you are buying something just to show off, or just to make yourself believe that you are worth something, then you are a slave. If you drive a Mercedes just for people to see that you are doing well in life while you cannot even pay your rent, you are a slave. Your worth does not depend on clothes, cars, houses, or anything when you are in Christ. Your worth comes from the fact that God loves you. Apostle Paul says it this way, *"But we have this treasure in earthen vessels, that the excellence of the power may be of God and not of us"* (1 Corinthians 4:17, NKJV). Do not waste your money on useless things. Instead, invest it. You are not a slave. You are a son.

Prayer

Creator of all things, thank You for the blessings in my life. I vow to be a son of good stewardship. In Jesus' name, I pray. Amen.

Application

Make a list of two non-essential and can go without items you will eliminate from your spending habit for the next six months, then at the end evaluate yourself to see how well you did.

Hearing the voice of God

_____

_____

_____

_____

_____

_____

_____

_____

_____

_____

_____

Bible in a year
1 King 17 - 1 King 18

April 20
A Slave Mentality Creates Distrust

<u>KEY VERSE</u>

"The field is the world, the good seeds are the sons of the kingdom, but the tares are the sons of the wicked one"
(Matthew 13:38, NKJV)

One of the great mischiefs of slavery is that it destroyed mutual trust among Black people. In Africa, the Black man was purchased by a white man, but he was not sold by a white man. Another black man sold him. As a result, early in his history, he has learned not to trust another black brother. We see that attitude of distrust everywhere. For instance, a Haitian proverb says, *"Depi nan Ginen nèg rayi nèg."* But there are others, *"Dan griyen ce danje," "Zanmi prè ce kouto de bò" "Jan Chat maché ce pa konsa li kembe rat" "Rann sèvis mennen chagrin"*, *"Nan kout men ou jwen kout pye."* All those sayings exude distrust. But where there is no trust, there is no love. Because love *"believes all things"* (1 Corinthians 13:7). When there is no love, there is no sense of family. Do you have a hard time trusting others, especially people in leadership? That's a slave mentality. Break out of it by the power of the Holy Ghost!

Prayer

Holy Spirit of God, I invoke Your infinite power in my life today. Spirit of distrust, I revoke you and replace you with a spirit of trust. In Jesus' Mighty name I pray. Amen.

Application

In what way, today, are you challenging yourself to always give to others the benefit of doubt?

Hearing the voice of God

_____

_____

_____

_____

_____

_____

_____

_____

_____

_____

Bible in a year
1 King 19 – 1 King 21

April 21

The Baptism of Love

KEY VERSE

"The field is the world, the good seeds are the sons of the kingdom, but the tares are the sons of the wicked one"

(Matthew 13:38, NKJV)

Most people do not realize that when John the Baptist dipped Jesus in the Jordan, He received three baptisms simultaneously.

First, He was baptized with water, which represents repentance. John the Baptist discerned quickly that Jesus did not need that baptism. He said, *"I should be baptized by You, and you come to me"* (Matthew 2:14, NKJV). The second baptism Jesus received was that of the Holy Ghost. The Bible states that as Jesus was coming out of the water, *"The Holy Spirit descended upon Him like a dove"* (Matt. 3:16, NKJV). From that moment on, He was endowed with power. The third baptism that He experienced was a baptism of love. This happened when the father's voice boomed from heaven and said, *"This is <u>My beloved</u> Son in Whom I am well-pleased"* (Matthew 3:17, NKJV). As a son, your heavenly Father wants to baptize you in His love today.

Prayer

Heavenly Father, let the water, the power, and the love that came upon Christ on the day of baptism, flow in my life today. Jesus, in Your mighty name I pray. Amen.

Application

What are some negative emotions you are working to overcome today as you usher into the divine love of God?

Hearing the voice of God

_____

_____

_____

_____

_____

_____

_____

_____

_____

_____

Bible in a year
1 King 22

April 22

What Does it Mean to be Baptized in Love?

<u>KEY VERSE</u>

"The field is the world, the good seeds are the sons of the kingdom, but the tares are the sons of the wicked one"
(Matthew 13:38, NKJV)

Jesus was baptized in water, the spirit, and love all at once. During His baptism, the Father said, *"This is my son in whom I am well-pleased"* (Matt. 3:17, NKJV). Notice that the Father declared those words regarding Jesus before He started preaching, healing the sick, casting out demons, and before He even died on the cross of Calvary. In other words, God's love was not contingent upon His performance. You are baptized in love when you have a deep inner conviction that God loves you just because you are His son or daughter. It's not because of what you have done or will do. God loves you regardless of your spiritual performance, which frees you to love Him in return. Your Heavenly Father loves you. Your spiritual father loves you too. Smile.

Prayer

Heavenly Father, every day I think of Your love for me. I want that thought to manifest in a smile. In Jesus' name, I pray. Amen.

Application

What kind of life transformation are you looking forward to experiencing as you freely receive the genuine love of both your heavenly and spiritual father?

Hearing the voice of God

_____
_____
_____
_____
_____
_____
_____
_____
_____
_____

Bible in a year
2 King 1 – 2 King 4

Secure in Father's love

KEY VERSE

"The field is the world, the good seeds are the sons of the kingdom, but the tares are the sons of the wicked one"

(Matthew 13:38, NKJV)

Jesus received three baptisms in the Jordan: water baptism for repentance, spirit baptism for power, and love baptism for identity. When you are baptized in God's love, become secure in who you are as a son. You are not afraid of losing God's love if you underperform or misbehave. Remember, love in the Bible is not primarily a sentimental word but an active one that denotes someone taking action for someone else's good. The conviction that we are loved keeps us stable in trying times. Thus, in his trials, Paul was able to write, *"What can separate us from the love of Christ? Shall tribulation or distress, or persecution, or famine...."* (Romans 8:35, NKJV). Then Paul went on to answer the question, *"Nothing shall separate us from the <u>Love of God</u>, which is Christ Jesus our Lord"* (Romans 8:39, NKJV). A son is secured in his Father's love even in the darkest moments. Let the love of God embrace you today.

Prayer

Father God, Your love I receive today. I pray in the name of my precious Lord and Savior, Jesus Christ. Amen.

Application

How do you plan to deal with the doubts and voices of the enemy that would otherwise mislead you from believing that you are truly loved by God?

Hearing the voice of God

_____

_____

_____

_____

_____

_____

_____

_____

_____

_____

Bible in a year
2 King 5 – 2 King 7

April 24

Convicted of God's Love

KEY VERSE

*"The field is the world, the good seeds are the sons of the king-
dom, but the tares are the sons of the wicked one"*
(Matthew 13:38, NKJV)

Jesus knew that the Father loved Him. Let's look at a
few verses witnessing the Father's affection and affini-
ty for the Son to prove this. John 3:35 states, *"The Father
loves the Son and has given all things into His hand"* (John 3:35,
NKJV). John 5:20 affirms, *"For the Father loves the Son, and
shows Him all things that He does; and He will show Him greater
works than these, that you may marvel"* (John 5:20, NKJV). In
John 17:24, Jesus prays, *"Father, I desire that they also whom
You gave Me may be with Me where I am, that they may behold My
glory which You have given Me; for You loved Me before the foundation of the world"* (John 17:24, NKJV). Do you know that
your Heavenly Father loves you? Do you know your spiritual
parents love you? Do you know your brothers and sisters
in Christ love you? Take some time to think of that love.

Prayer

Father God, today, I embrace your love, the love of my spiritual parents, and the love of my brothers and sisters. In Jesus' name, I am loved. Amen.

Application

How will you begin to utilize the power of love that you are receiving from every angle to change your own perspective about other people?

Hearing the voice of God

_____

_____

_____

_____

_____

_____

_____

_____

_____

_____

Bible in a year
2 King 8 – 2 King 9

April 25

Love as the Ground Motive

KEY VERSE

"The field is the world, the good seeds are the sons of the king-
dom, but the tares are the sons of the wicked one"
(Matthew 13:38, NKJV)

When you know that God loves you, loving Him and loving
others becomes a natural reaction. The Apostle John says,
"We love Him because He first loved us" (1 John 4:19, NKJV).
Knowing that God loves you makes it easier to love God and
others. Let the love of God for you and your love for God
and others be the ground motive of everything you do in life.

Prayer

King of kings, may my every action in Your kingdom be in-
spired by love. In Jesus' name, I pray. Amen.

Application

Being convinced that God was the initiator in the love affair established with Him, how does this reality help you against trying to live out performances in order to be loved?

Hearing the voice of God

_____

_____

_____

_____

_____

_____

_____

_____

_____

_____

Bible in a year
2 King 10 – 2 King 13

April 26

The Son Died out of Love

KEY VERSE

"The field is the world, the good seeds are the sons of the king-dom, but the tares are the sons of the wicked one"
(Matthew 13:38, NKJV)

Overcome by the Father's love, Jesus surrendered Himself to die. He said to his disciples, *"Greater love has no one than this, that someone lay down his life for his friends"* (John 15:13, NKJV). When Jesus sweated blood in the garden of Gethsemane, it was love. When He endured thirty-nine blows on his back, it was love. When He stretched out his hands and feet to be pierced, it was love. When He bent down his head to receive a crown of thorns, it was love. Love caused Him to sacrifice Himself for us. Love should also cause us to sacrifice for Him. What are you willing to give up to do the will of Christ?

Prayer

My Lord and Savior, thank you for Your proven love. In Your name, I pray. Amen.

Application

Love is sacrificial. What do you feel God is asking you to forsake today as you freely embrace His love?

Hearing the voice of God

_____

_____

_____

_____

_____

_____

_____

_____

_____

_____

Bible in a year
2 King 14 – 2 King 16

April 27

To love, We Must Die to Ourselves

KEY VERSE

"The field is the world, the good seeds are the sons of the kingdom, but the tares are the sons of the wicked one"
(Matthew 13:38, NKJV)

We cannot love God and others fully until we have died to ourselves. Jesus had to die to himself in the garden of Gethsemane and said to the Father, *"Not my will, but yours"* (Luke 22:42). Likewise, if you are going to love others, you learn to die to yourself. The ego is the greatest enemy of love. Ego pushes you to focus on yourself; love pushes you to focus on others. Those two forces go in two different directions. This is why the Bible states, *"Love is not selfish"* (1 Corinthians 13:5-7). To love like a son, we must say every day like the Apostle Paul, *"I have been crucified with Christ; it is no longer I who live, but Christ lives in me; and the life which I now live in the flesh I live by faith in the Son of God, who loved me and gave Himself for me"* (Galatians 2:20, NKJV). Ask God to show which area of your life you need to die.

Prayer

Holy Spirit, my friend and guide, show me which area in my life needs to die so that love can thrive. I pray in the name of my Lord and Savior. Amen.

Application

In what area(s) will you be practicing dying today, and why do you choose that specific area?

Hearing the voice of God

_____

_____

_____

_____

_____

_____

_____

_____

_____

_____

Bible in a year
2 King 17 – 2 King 18

April 28
Love Will Make You Look Like Your Father

KEY VERSE

"The field is the world, the good seeds are the sons of the kingdom, but the tares are the sons of the wicked one"
(Matthew 13:38, NKJV)

As sons of God, we must look like Him. We must love. The God we serve is both a God of faith and love. He spoke to nothingness and said, let there be light, and it came to pass. That was faith. This is why Jesus says, *"Have the faith of God"* (Mark 10:11, YLT; French, NSLG). In His love, He sent His one and only Son Jesus to die for us (John 3:16). Of the two virtues, which is the greatest? Love. Faith makes us act like God, but love makes us look like God. This is why the Apostle John writes, *"Love has been perfected among us in this: that we may have boldness in the day of judgment; because as He is, so are we in this world."* (1 John. 4:17, NKJV). It is love that makes us look like God's sons in this world. We all need to ask ourselves: Who do we look like when we think, speak, and act in this world? We should further ask ourselves: Who do we want to look like? Ponder those questions for a moment.

Prayer

Lord Jesus, as I prayerfully go through my day, help me to think on these questions and I ask for Your revelation. Amen.

Application

What are some behaviors you will need to adapt in order to look more and more like Christ, and also, what needs to be forsaken?

Hearing the voice of God

_____

_____

_____

_____

_____

_____

_____

_____

_____

_____

Bible in a year
2 King 19 – 2 King 21

April 29
Love Will Make You a Perfect Son

KEY VERSE
"The field is the world, the good seeds are the sons of the kingdom, but the tares are the sons of the wicked one"
(Matthew 13:38, NKJV)

We have often been taught that it is impossible to have a perfect Christian life, and this is true. However, we can have moments of perfection. As sons, Jesus said to us, *"Be perfect as your heavenly Father is perfect"* (Matt. 5:48, NIV). What allows us to operate at the level of perfection in certain moments of our lives is when our thoughts and words are only motivated by one thing: the Love of God. *"But above all these things put on love, which is the bond of perfection"* (Col. 3:14, NKJV). We should image the bond that Paul is speaking about here as a bridge that takes us to the land of perfection. Perfection is possible—at least momentarily. The vehicle that takes us there is love. Think love. Speak love. Live love. It helps you to reflect on the perfection of your Father in Heaven.

Prayer
Father God, I am not perfect, but I seek your perfection. I desire for my thoughts to think love, my words to speak love, and my life to live love. In Jesus' name, I pray. Amen.

Application

How are you going to practice speaking, thinking, and living out the love of God in your own life today?

Hearing the voice of God

Bible in a year
2 King 22 – 2 King 25

April 30

Love Opens the Vault of God's Blessings

KEY VERSE

"The field is the world, the good seeds are the sons of the king-dom, but the tares are the sons of the wicked one"
(Matthew 13:38, NKJV)

Love affects God's blessings in our lives. If a father has a 12-year-old boy who does not know how to drive, he would never hand over his car key to him so he can take it to the street. He would not do that because the son is not ready to enjoy that kind of privilege. There are many privileges in God. However, God hands them over to us as we mature in the faith to handle them properly. The Apostle Paul explains it in those words, *"Now I say that the heir, as long as he is a child, does not differ at all from a slave, though he is master of all"* (Galatians 4:1, NKJV). As heirs of God, we have all access to all the riches of God; however, these graces will only become available to us as we mature in the faith. Some people are asking for a marriage who are not ready for it. Some people are asking for a promotion at work who are not prepared for it. Some people are asking for a ministry who are not ready for it. God, in His love, will always shield us from the blessings that He knows might destroy us. What makes us mature enough to handle God's blessings? Love. If you want to enjoy God's blessings, then as a son, you must love. Do everything out of love for God and your spiritual family.

Prayer

Holy Spirit of God, fill my heart with love. In the Lord Jesus Christ's name, I pray. Amen.

Application

In what area of your life will you need to practice patience as God's love is being made perfect in you?

Hearing the voice of God

_____

_____

_____

_____

_____

_____

_____

_____

_____

_____

Bible in a year
1 Chronicles 1

"Sonship is a matter of the heart. Don't confuse closeness with connectedness"

Gregory Toussaint

May 1st

A Son is Connected

KEY VERSE

"The field is the world, the good seeds are the sons of the king-dom, but the tares are the sons of the wicked one"
(Matthew 13:38, NKJV)

A slave interacts with a father, but is not connected with him. A son, on the other hand, is connected. Jesus was so connected with His Heavenly Father that He said, *"My Father and I are one"* (John 10:30, NKJV). One time, Jesus Christ was talking about the Father; Philip said to Him, *"Lord, show us the Father, and it is sufficient for us"* (John 14:8, NKJV). Jesus answered Philip, *"Have I been with you so long, and yet you have not known Me, Philip? He who has seen Me has seen the Father"* (John 14:9, NKJV). Jesus Christ was so inextricably linked to the Father that to see Him was to see the Father. Likewise, a spiritual son is connected with his father. As a member of the family, do you feel connected?

Prayer

Christ my Lord and Savior, per the ability You have to be one with the Father, I pray for that grace today in Your name. Amen.

Application

In what ways do you wish that your mindset would be similar to your spiritual father, and what are you doing now in order to adapt?

Hearing the voice of God

_____

_____

_____

_____

_____

_____

_____

_____

_____

_____

_____

Bible in a year
1 Chronicles 2 - 1 Chronicles 3

May 2
Sonship is a matter of the heart

KEY VERSE
"The field is the world, the good seeds are the sons of the kingdom, but the tares are the sons of the wicked one"
(Matthew 13:38, NKJV)

Some might ask, how can I connect with a spiritual father if I am not close to him? Sonship is not a matter of proximity. It is a matter of the heart. The Lord said, *"He will turn the <u>heart of fathers</u> to their sons, and the <u>heart of sons</u> to their fathers"* (Malachi 4:6, NABRE//DRB). Spiritual connection has to do with the direction of the heart. How do you feel about your spiritual father in your heart? Many years ago, a pastor visited me and told me, "Do not neglect the sons that are far away. They will be among the best that you will have." At that moment, I was being introduced to the notion of sonship, and I didn't fully understand what he meant. Over time, I have come to realize that it was pure truth. I have had people in my inner circle who were not sons, and I have had people from far who have been true sons. Sonship is a matter of the heart. Do not confuse proximity with connectivity. Proximity is of the flesh, while connectivity is of the spirit or "heart."

Furthermore, I have realized that the more someone connects on the physical level, the more difficult it is for them to connect spiritually. Just because you are close does not mean that you are a son, and, being far does not mean that you are not a son. Sonship has nothing to do with proximity but everything with the heart. Are you a son?

Prayer

Father God, help me to fully understand the notion of proximity versus connectivity. In Christ's name, I pray. Amen.

Application

What are you doing now or will begin to do in order to create a spiritual connection with your spiritual father?

Hearing the voice of God

_____

_____

_____

_____

_____

_____

_____

_____

_____

_____

Bible in a year
1 Chronicles 4:1 - 1 Chronicles 6:30

May 3

Sonship is a Matter of the Spirit

KEY VERSE

"The field is the world, the good seeds are the sons of the kingdom, but the tares are the sons of the wicked one"
(Matthew 13:38, NKJV)

The prophet, Malachi, teaches us that sonship is a matter of the heart. What does he mean by heart? The "heart" in the Bible means "the deepest part of something." For example, when we want to talk about the deepest part of the sea, we say "the heart of the sea." When we get to the most important part of a subject, we say we are at "the heart of the subject." Thus, when the Bible is referring to your heart, it means the most important part of you or your inner self.

Now, what is the most important part of you? The apostle Paul answers that question by listing the three different parts of men in order of priority. He says, *"Now may the God of peace Himself sanctify you completely; and may your whole spirit, soul, and body be preserved blameless at the coming of our Lord Jesus Christ"* (1 Thessalonians 5:23, NKJV). Notice that he mentioned first the spirit, then the soul, and lastly, the body. The spirit is the deepest and most important part of man. This is why it is often used synonymously with heart. David says, *"The LORD is near to those who have a broken heart, And saves such as have a contrite spirit"* (Psalm 34:18, NKJV). In this text, a "broken heart" is synonymous with a "contrite spirit." He says further on, *"Create in me a clean heart, O God,*

And renew a steadfast spirit within me" (Psalm 51:10, NKJV). Again we see that a "clean heart" is in alignment with a "steadfast spirit." He also says, "*I call to remembrance my song in the night; I meditate within my heart, And my spirit makes diligent search.*" (Psalm 77:6, NKJV). To meditate in one's heart is to search one's spirit. Thus, when the Lord says, "*He will turn the heart of fathers to their sons, and the heart of sons to their fathers*" (Malachi 3:24, NABRE//DRB), it means that He will turn the spirit of the fathers to the sons and the spirit of the sons to their fathers. Sonship is not a physical connection, which happens, through proximity, but a spiritual connection, which occurs in the heart. Since the spirit has no boundary, wherever you are, you can be a genuine son and still enjoy all of the spiritual benefits of s son.

Prayer

Father God, renew my spirit today. I long for the heart of a true son. In Jesus Christ's name, I pray. Amen.

Application

How could a spiritual connection to your spiritual father be beneficial to you, and what are you doing daily to establish such connection?

Hearing the voice of God

_____

_____

_____

_____

_____

_____

_____

_____

_____

_____

_____

Bible in a year
1 Chronicles 6:31 - 1 Chronicles 7:40

May 4
A Son Carries the Father's Spirit

KEY VERSE

"The field is the world, the good seeds are the sons of the king-dom, but the tares are the sons of the wicked one"
(Matthew 13:38, NKJV)

Sonship, is a spiritual connection. What does it mean to be connected with a spiritual father? First, it means to have the same spirit. Moses had served Israel for many years. He arrived at a point where he felt he could no longer work by himself. He asked the Lord for help. The Lord told him to choose 70 men of good reputation among the children of Israel. Then He said, *"I will come down and talk with you there. I will take of the Spirit that is upon you and will put the same upon them, and they shall bear the burden of the people with you, that you may not bear it yourself alone"* (Numbers 11:17, NKJV). Notice that God's first requirement for the men who were going to help Moses bear the burden was to have his spirit. Now, what did it mean by having Moses' spirit? Did God take Moses' human Spirit and give it to the 70 elders? No! If He did, Moses would have died. When a person's spirit leaves his body, he dies (Ecc. 12:7; Luke 23:46). Having Moses' spirit, just like Elijah's spirit (Luke 1:15-17), meant that they had the same manifestation of the Holy Spirit in his life.

The Holy Spirit is one river with different streams or operations (Psalm 46:4). A son flows in the same stream as the father.

Prayer

God of Grace and Mercy, direct me to the same stream as my spiritual father. In Jesus' name, I pray. Amen.

Application

In what way are you going to help your spiritual father carry the burden God has laid on him, and how can you begin to do that today?

Hearing the voice of God

_____

_____

_____

_____

_____

_____

_____

_____

_____

_____

Bible in a year
1 Chronicles 8 - 1 Chronicles 9

May 5
How to Receive a Father's Spirit? - Pray

KEY VERSE

*"The field is the world, the good seeds are the sons of the king-
dom, but the tares are the sons of the wicked one"*
(Matthew 13:38, NKJV)

One may wonder, "How does a son receive his father's spirit?" First, you must pray for it. Notice that the Lord said,
*"Then I will come down and talk with you there. I will take of the
Spirit that is upon you and will put the same upon them; and they
shall bear the burden of the people with you, that you may not bear it
yourself alone"* (Num. 11:17, NKJ). Notice that the word "**I**"
is repeated many times. In other words, it is God Himself
who takes the father's spirit and puts it on the son. It is not
a man-made transaction. A father cannot do it himself. He
can pray for his son, but God must approve the transaction
for any transfer to occur. When you go to a store to make a
purchase, you swipe your credit card at the counter, but you
cannot walk out with the items unless the bank approves
the transaction. The bank is the one that transfers the funds
from your account to your vendor's account. Likewise, in
order for any spiritual transfer to happen, the bank of heav-
en must approve. The father is the one who transfers the
anointing from one person to another. This is why it is important to pray for a father's anointing.

Prayer

The God of all spirit and flesh, it is my desire to be of one spirit with my spiritual father. Let this prayer be your perfect will. In Christ Jesus, I pray. Amen.

Application

How much time will you begin to put aside to pray for your spiritual father's anointing, and why is that important to you?

Hearing the voice of God

_____

_____

_____

_____

_____

_____

_____

_____

_____

_____

Bible in a year
1 Chronicles 10 - 1 Chronicles 12

May 6

How to Receive a Father's Spirit? - Listen

KEY VERSE

"The field is the world, the good seeds are the sons of the kingdom, but the tares are the sons of the wicked one"
(Matthew 13:38, NKJV)

The second discipline that will enable you to receive a father's anointing is to listen constantly to his words. Jesus explains to us why words are so important. He says, *"It is the Spirit who gives life; the flesh profits nothing. The words that I speak to you are spirit, and they are life"* (John 6:63, NKJV). Words are both "spirit" and "life." Thus, by listening to a father's words, you are connected to his "spirit" and his "life." When God sent Peter to Cornelius' house, he gathered the group and started preaching. The Bible says, *"While Peter was still speaking these words, the Holy Spirit fell upon all those who heard the word"* (Acts 10:44, NKJV). Notice that the Holy Spirit did not fill everyone but on those who heard. The anointing of the Holy Spirit flowed through the words.

Prayer

Holy Spirit of God, let the words that are coming out of my spiritual father's mouth penetrate my inner self and transform my life. In Jesus' name, I pray. Amen.

Application

What will you begin to do to listen more effectively to the words of your spiritual father?

Hearing the voice of God

_____

_____

_____

_____

_____

_____

_____

_____

_____

_____

Bible in a year
1 Chronicles 13 - 1 Chronicles 16

May 7

How to Receive a Father's Spirit? - Open your Heart

<u>**KEY VERSE**</u>

"The field is the world, the good seeds are the sons of the kingdom, but the tares are the sons of the wicked one"

(Matthew 13:38, NKJV)

For a transfer of anointing to happen, you must not only listen, but you must also receive. Thus, the Word says, *"Son of man, receive into your heart all My words that I speak to you, and heart with your ears"* (Ezekiel 3:10, NKJV). You can hear with your ears and not receive in your heart. For a spiritual transfer to happen, both elements need to be present. Here is a little practical advice. First, make sure you do your devotion every day. Second, listen to the Sunday sermon at least once a week. Third, find old series and start listening to them. The most important thing;however, is to listen with your heart.

Prayer

Lord, I open my heart to receive. Thank you for the practical advice I was given today. Help me to be disciplined as I am applying them. In the mighty name of Jesus Christ, I pray. Amen.

Application

What can you do to better prepare your heart the next time you have a chance to listen to your spiritual father's instructions?

Hearing the voice of God

_____

_____

_____

_____

_____

_____

_____

_____

_____

_____

Bible in a year
1 Chronicles 17 - 1 Chronicles 19

May 8
A Son Thinks his Father's Thoughts

KEY VERSE

"The field is the world, the good seeds are the sons of the king-dom, but the tares are the sons of the wicked one"
(Matthew 13:38, NKJV)

Being connected with a spiritual father not only means to have the same spirit, but it also means to have the same mind. Paul said this regarding his spiritual son. *"And I hope in the Lord Jesus to send Timothy unto you shortly, that I also may be of good comfort, when I know the things concerning you. For I have no man so of the same mind…"* (Philippians 2:19, DRA). Timothy had the same mind as Paul. We are all different. One may wonder, how does someone have the same mind as another? Agreeing is not automatic; it is a decision. Hence, Paul writes the Corinthians, *"Finally, brethren, farewell. Become complete. Be of good comfort, <u>be of one mind</u>, live in peace; and the God of love and peace will be with you"* (2 Corinthians 13:11, NKJV). When I had just started my Christian walk, I had a spiritual father named Pastor Thomas Jean-Baptiste. He was a man who was known for his wisdom. When I was asked a question, I would often ask in my heart. "How would Pastor Thomas answer that question?" Suddenly, I could think of myself as a wise sixty-year-old man instead of a foolish sixteen year old teenager. I had to consciously make the decision. That conscious choice connected me to the anointed wisdom that rested upon his life.

Prayer

God of wisdom, I pray to be of one mind with my spiritual father. In Jesus Christ's name, I pray. Amen.

Application

In what area right now or in the future will you utilize your spiritual father's reasoning in order to make challenging decisions?

Hearing the voice of God

_____

_____

_____

_____

_____

_____

_____

_____

_____

_____

Bible in a year
1 Chronicles 20 - 1 Chronicles 23

May 9
A Son Feels his Father's Emotions

KEY VERSE

"The field is the world, the good seeds are the sons of the king-dom, but the tares are the sons of the wicked one"
(Matthew 13:38, NKJV)

To be connected with a spiritual father does not only mean to have the same spirit and mind, but it also means to have the same feelings. The Darby *translation of Paul's recommen-dation to Timothy says, "I will send you Timothy, For I have no one like-minded who will care with <u>genuine feeling</u> how ye get on"* (Philippians 2:20, DRBY). To be a true son, you must be able to feel what a father feels. Hosea was a prophet in Israel. One day God called him and asked him to marry a prostitute. Astounded, he heeded to the voice of the Lord. He took in and married a prostitute by the name of Gomer. He had two children with her. Then, after a while, Gomer gets up and goes back to the life of prostitution. The Lord, *"Go again, <u>love a woman who is loved</u> by a lover and is <u>committing adultery,</u> just like the love of the LORD for the children of Israel, who look to other gods and love the raisin cakes of the pagans"* (Hoseah 3:1, NKJV).

You might be thinking, "Why was God so cruel towards Hoseah?" God was not cruel. Israel had committed spiritual adultery towards God by serving idols; despite that, God loved her. Hoseah was God's representative whose responsibility was to deliver the message. He could not deliver a message of love in spite of betrayal if he had not himself experienced the emotion. A son represents a father. He cannot do that well if he does not feel what the father feels. Timothy felt what Paul felt. As a son, you need to pay attention to what your Heavenly and spiritual father loves and hates. When you face a situation, you need to ask how my Heavenly Father and spiritual father feel about this?

Prayer

Christ, my Lord, I pray for a calm and thoughtful heart. In every situation, I want to be able to stop and acknowledge You and discern what my spiritual father would do. In your name, I pray. Amen.

Application

Have you taken a decision in the past about something that is contrary to one your spiritual father would have taken. How will you handle similar matters in the future?

Hearing the voice of God

_____

_____

_____

_____

_____

_____

_____

_____

_____

Bible in a year
1 Chronicles 24 - 1 Chronicles 26

May 10

A Son Execute His Father's Will

KEY VERSE

"The field is the world, the good seeds are the sons of the king-dom, but the tares are the sons of the wicked one"
(Matthew 13:38, NKJV)

Finally, a son not only has the spirit, mind, and feelings of his father; he also has the same will. After Paul had said that he would send Timothy because there is none like him, he added, *"For all seek their own, not the things which are of Christ Jesus. But you know his proven character, that as a son with his father he served with me in the gospel."* (Philippians 2:21–22, NKJV). Timothy, as a son, was not seeking to do his own will, but Paul's. In doing so, he was also serving Christ. He had a common will with this spiritual father and had a common will with Christ.

Jesus was the first one to illustrate that principle. He said, *"For I have come down from heaven, not to do My own will, but the will of Him who sent Me. This is the will of the Father who sent Me..."* (John 6:38–39, NKJV). A son executes his father's will. How faithful have you been in executing different directions that have been given to you?

Prayer

Holy Spirit of God, You who search and know my inner-most, help me to answer these questions today: How deep is my attachment with my spiritual family? How deep is my attachment to my spiritual parents? In Christ's name, I seek your counsel. Amen.

Application

How are your own will and goals different to that of your spiritual father, and how do you plan to surrender your own goals to embrace those of your spiritual father?

Hearing the voice of God

_____

_____

_____

_____

_____

_____

_____

_____

_____

_____

Bible in a year
1 Chronicles 27 - 1 Chronicles 29

May 11
The Biggest Hindrance to Sonship

<u>KEY VERSE</u>
"The field is the world, the good seeds are the sons of the king-dom, but the tares are the sons of the wicked one"
(Matthew 13:38, NKJV)

The biggest hindrance to sonship, or spiritual connection, is self-interest. When Paul wanted someone to send to Philippi, he said he could not find anyone except Timothy. He then stated the reason: *"For all <u>seek their own</u>, not the things which are of Christ Jesus. <u>But you</u> know his proven character, that as <u>a son</u> with his <u>father</u> he served with me in the gospel"* (Philippians 2:21-22, NKJV). Self-will is the biggest reason it is difficult for people to connect as sons. If you seek to further your interest or execute your agenda, either in the short or the long term, you will never be a true son. The self-interest and self-will you have in your heart will not allow you to connect fully.

Prayer
Holy Spirit of God, is self-will or self-interest blocking me from becoming a true son? I seek your revelation today. In Jesus' name, I pray. Amen.

Application

Ask the Holy Spirit to show you any areas in your life where self-interest conflicts with sonship.

Hearing the voice of God

_____
_____
_____
_____
_____
_____
_____
_____
_____
_____

Bible in a year
2 Chronicles 1:1 - 2 Chronicles 5:1

May 12

The Secret of True Sonship

KEY VERSE

"The field is the world, the good seeds are the sons of the king-dom, but the tares are the sons of the wicked one"

(Matthew 13:38, NKJV)

The secret of true sonship is to die to oneself. He said to them all, *"If anyone desires to come after Me, let him deny himself, and take up his cross daily, and follow Me"* (Luke 9:23, NKJV). Only after you have given yourself fully to your Heavenly Father can you give yourself to your spiritual father. Sonship we said is a cross but for every cross, there is the crown; for every crucifixion, there is a resurrection. Paul says, *"They first gave themselves to the Lord, and then to us by the will of God"* (2 Corinthians. 8:5, NKJV). Notice they gave themselves to the Lord first, then to Paul.

Prayer

Father God, I surrender fully to your hands and I commit to the vision You have given to my spiritual father. For the advancement of Your kingdom, I pray. Amen.

Application

In what area do you still feel that you need to completely practice surrendering, first to the Lord then to your spiritual father?

Hearing the voice of God

Bible in a year
2 Chronicles 5:2 - 2 Chronicles 7:22

May 13
Natural Slavery Destroyed the Sense of Family

KEY VERSE
"The field is the world, the good seeds are the sons of the kingdom, but the tares are the sons of the wicked one"
(Matthew 13:38, NKJV)

One of the big differences between a son and a slave is that the son has a sense of belonging, but the slave does not. To understand that mystery, first, we must look at it from a historical standpoint. During the trans-Atlantic slave trade, slaves were often bought as families in the ports of Africa. However, they would often separate when they arrived in the Americas. The father, mother, and children would often be sold to a different vendor. As a result, slaves learned not to attach themselves out of fear of separation. Moreover, slaves who fell in love while in the plantations were not married. To make matters worse, even though slaves were not allowed to marry each other, they were encouraged to have children because those children would be considered properties of the master as well. All of these tragic misfortunes contribute to a weakening of family bonds. Thus, people with a slave mentality have difficulty valuing family bonds. How much do you value your family? How much do you value your marriage? How much do you value your children? How much do you value your extended family members?

Prayer

Lord, God Almighty, I come in Your name and break the slave mentality operating in my life. I am a true son. In Jesus' name, I pray. Amen.

Application

Reflect on the different ways you could value your family more today, then begin with the small things.

Hearing the voice of God

_____

_____

_____

_____

_____

_____

_____

_____

_____

_____

Bible in a year
2 Chronicles 8 - 2 Chronicles 11

May 14
Spiritual Slavery Destroys the Sense of Family

KEY VERSE

"The field is the world, the good seeds are the sons of the kingdom, but the tares are the sons of the wicked one"
(Matthew 13:38, NKJV)

Like physical slavery, spiritual servitude destroys family bonds. As long as Adam and Eve were walking in obedience, they lived in harmony with each other. But the day that they decided to disobey the Lord, disharmony was introduced into their family lives. As a result, Adam sinned, and God asked him why he ate the forbidden fruit? He responded, *"The woman whom You gave to be with me, she gave me of the tree, and I ate"* (Genesis 3:12, NKJV). As soon as Adam sinned against God, he started to have marriage problems. He was blaming his wife for his shortcomings. Later on, in the book of Genesis, we are told the story of evil in Cain. Cain became jealous of his brother. When God asked him about his brother, his response was: *"Am I my brother's keeper?"* (Genesis 4:9, NKJV). As long as Adam was living as a son, his family was intact, but when he became a slave, the family bond between himself and Eve started to break down. The gospel restores our sense of family. Thus, the Bible states, *"So then you are no longer strangers and aliens, but you are fellow citizens with the saints and <u>members of the household of God</u>"* (Ephesians 2:19, NKJV). How much do you value your spiritual family?

Prayer

Father God, I thank you for my spiritual parents and I bless your name for my brothers and sisters. Help me to understand the importance of being part of a spiritual family. In Jesus' name, I pray. Amen.

Application

In what area(s) today can you improve and enhance the relationships you have created with your spiritual family?

Hearing the voice of God

_____

_____

_____

_____

_____

_____

_____

_____

_____

_____

Bible in a year
2 Chronicles 12 - 2 Chronicles 15

The Son Remains in the House

KEY VERSE

"The field is the world, the good seeds are the sons of the kingdom, but the tares are the sons of the wicked one"
(Matthew 13:38, NKJV)

Slaves do not have a sense of family. It is not difficult to spot those who carry such a mentality in the body of Christ. All you have to do is observe their reaction when they are offended. Some people will leave their small group, ministry, or church if someone rubs them the wrong way. If an usher fails to receive them properly at the entrance, they turn right back to the car and leave. They have no attachment to their spiritual family. Sons, on the other hand, are attached. This is why Jesus said, *"A slave does not abide in the house forever, but a son abides forever"* (John 8:35, NKJV).

I grew up in a large family composed of four boys and four girls. All four of us boys used to take karate lessons. When we came home from class, we would often practice with each other. But what would start as a make-believe fight often turned into a serious one? In the process, we would get angry, and we would push, punch, and kick each other. But when it was all over, we would sit together and watch a nice movie. None of us thought about leaving the house. We remained in the family because we were not slaves but sons. Is running away the first thing that crosses your mind when you're offended at church? If this is the case, it is a slave mentality. You need to ask God to help you break it.

Prayer

Father God, help me to break any slave mentality that is keeping me from being a true son. In Your son Jesus Christ name, I pray. Amen.

Application

With running away not being an option for legitimate sons, what will be your new way of handling conflicts you will likely have with members of your spiritual family?

Hearing the voice of God

_____
_____
_____
_____
_____
_____
_____
_____
_____
_____

Bible in a year
2 Chronicles 16 - 2 Chronicles 19

What is Loyalty?

KEY VERSE

"The field is the world, the good seeds are the sons of the king-dom, but the tares are the sons of the wicked one"

(Matthew 13:38, NKJV)

Slaves have no sense of belonging and , therefore, are not loyal. On the other hand, sons are. Loyalty is a manifestation of faithfulness. When you are faithful to your work, it's called diligence. When you have faith in a cause, it is called commitment. When you are faithful to a person, it is called loyalty. In English, the word loyal is the translation of the Hebrew word "shalem," which is related to "shalom." It means whole, complete, perfect; it also means "sure," "peaceful," and "at rest." To be loyal means to give yourself wholly, completely, and perfectly to another; as a result, that person can be sure, peaceful, and at rest around you. Loyalty is a call to martyrdom. This is why Jesus said to his disciples, *"If anyone desires to come after Me, let him deny himself, and take up his cross daily, and follow Me"* (Luke 9:23, NKJV). Because *"No one can serve two masters; for either he will hate the one and love the other, or else he will be loyal to the one and despise the other..."* (Matthew 6:24, NKJV). To be loyal to your heavenly Father requires dying to your desires, ambitions, projects, and interests. Being loyal to a spiritual father requires the same. Thus, Paul, speaking of the Christians of Thessalonica, said, *"... They first gave themselves to the Lord, and then to us by the will of God"* (2 Corinthians 8:5, NKJV). When you have to choose between your interest and the kingdom? Which one do you choose? When you have to choose between your projects and the kingdom, which one do you choose?

Prayer

Lord, I desire to be loyal to the vision you have given to my spiritual father. Teach me how to effectively exercise my loyalty. In Jesus' name, I pray. Amen.

Application

What are some self desires you feel you have to give up today in order to embrace those of the kingdom, and where will you begin today?

Hearing the voice of God

_____

_____

_____

_____

_____

_____

_____

_____

_____

_____

Bible in a year
2 Chronicles 20 - 2 Chronicles 23

May 17

Make a Name

KEY VERSE
*"The field is the world, the good seeds are the sons of the king-
dom, but the tares are the sons of the wicked one"*
(Matthew 13:38, NKJV)

Sometimes the best way to understand the concept is to an-
alyze its opposite. This is the approach that we wish to take
in explaining loyalty. Hence, let's look at the characteristics
of disloyalty.

The first mark of a disloyal person is the desire to build
a name. The story of Joab illustrates that very well in the Bible. He was a general in David's army and the king had sent
him to war to find the people of Ammon. He captured Rabbah, the royal city, and sent messengers to the King *"I have
fought against Rabbah, and I have taken the city's water supply. Now,
therefore, gather the rest of the people together and encamp against the
city and take it, lest I take the city and it is called after my name"*
(2 Samuel 12:26–28, NKJV). It was common for kings to
name a city they conquered after themselves in antiquity.
That's why we have places like Caesarea, Philippi, and Al-
exandria. These cities were named after Cesar, Philip, and
Alexander the Great. So what Joab was saying was that he
had conquered the city after himself. It appears to be a noble
gesture, but in reality, it was disloyalty cloaked in humility.
Joab was not the king. Therefore, the thought of naming
the city after him should not have even crossed his mind.
The simple fact is that he did reveal the disloyalty that sat in

his heart. This is why Joab is portrayed as a disloyal servant in the Bible. As a disloyal servant, Joab wanted to put his name to the city that he had conquered. Disloyal people in a house want to put their name on everything they do. They always want to be validated, recognized, thanked, and mentioned for the work that they have done. If they clean the church, they want everyone to know that they came in the middle of the night and did it. Disloyal people work for credit. Sons work for the welfare of the house, whether they are acknowledged or not.

Prayer

Father God, in all that I do, help me to elevate your name instead of mine. In Christ's name, I pray. Amen.

Application

How will you begin to adapt selflessness in the thing(s) you are currently doing for the Lord? How can it be more about the kingdom and less about you?

Hearing the voice of God

_____

_____

_____

_____

_____

_____

_____

_____

_____

_____

Bible in a year
2 Chronicles 24 - 2 Chronicles 26

May 18

Personal Gain

KEY VERSE
"The field is the world, the good seeds are the sons of the kingdom, but the tares are the sons of the wicked one"
(Matthew 13:38, NKJV)

Another mark of disloyalty is to serve for personal gain. For example, Naaman had sickness and came to Elisha for healing. Elisha told him to dip himself seven times into the Jordan, and he did. When he was done, his skin was restored. Then he offered the gift to Elisha, but the prophet refused. When the servant noticed that Naaman was leaving, he said to himself. *"Look, my master has spared Naaman this Syrian, while not receiving from his hands what he brought; but as the LORD lives, I will run after him and take <u>something from him</u>"* (2 Kings 5:20, NKJV). Notice the expression "I will run after him and take something from him." Naaman was serving for "something;" he was serving for personal gain.

A disloyal person serves to benefit something. Sometimes, it may not be money. It may simply be a connection. I once had a secretary in our ministry whom I asked to invite a guest artist to the church. She exchanged info with the guest. Before I knew it, she left the position at the church and became the guest's secretary. Some people search for connections, others for compliments and visibility, but sons serve for the pure pleasure of the serving because that is their house.

In the process of seeking advantages, people with a slave mentality often miss God's timing. When Gehazi came back from defending Naaman, Elisha said to Naaman, "*Is it time to receive money and to receive clothing, olive groves, and vineyards, sheep and oxen, male and female servants?*" (2 Kings 5:26, NKJV). In other words, the time to have clothing, olive groves, vineyards, sheep, oxen, and servants would come, but you've missed it. Now your lot is leprosy. Search deeply and ask yourself, "Why am I serving in ministry?"

Prayer

Holy Spirit, You who know my thoughts and search my inner being, help me to answer that question truthfully. In Jesus' name, I pray. Amen.

Application

How would you evaluate the service you render in the ministry? What is your purpose and intention for serving?

Hearing the voice of God

_____

_____

_____

_____

_____

_____

_____

_____

_____

_____

_____

Bible in a year
2 Chronicles 27 - 2 Chronicles 30

May 19

Hiding Important Info

KEY VERSE
"The field is the world, the good seeds are the sons of the kingdom, but the tares are the sons of the wicked one"
(Matthew 13:38, NKJV)

Another sign of disloyalty is hiding important information that can be detrimental to the house. No leader needs to know about every problem in an organization; however certain problems can threaten the organization's existence that they should know about. A person who has this information and hides them is disloyal. When something is going wrong in the spiritual family, God squarely puts the responsibility on the shoulders of those who know alert after they have done their part, those in authority. When there was contention in Corinth. Paul wrote, *"It has been declared to me concerning you, my brethren, by those of Chloe's household, that there are contentions among you"* (1 Corinthians 1:11, NKJV). Notice, the family of Chloe took the responsibility to let Paul know that there was a problem of division in the Corinthian church. And they did not do so with an anonymous letter. They identified themselves. Alerting authorities when there is a crisis pending is a sign of loyalty. It is also the duty of a son.

Prayer

Lord God, I pray for discernment in order to make right judgments. In your name, I pray. Amen.

Application

In what ways do you commit to protecting the ministry you are serving under today?

Hearing the voice of God

_____
_____
_____
_____
_____
_____
_____
_____
_____
_____

Bible in a year
2 Chronicles 31 - 2 Chronicles 33

May 20

Abandonment in Hard Times

KEY VERSE

"The field is the world, the good seeds are the sons of the king-dom, but the tares are the sons of the wicked one"
(Matthew 13:38, NKJV)

Another mark of disloyalty is abandonment in difficult times. Paul had wrought many miracles in his ministry and he had a large following. However, Paul enjoyed those companies as long as things were going well for him. When they arrested him, all of his friends abandoned him. He wrote to Timothy saying, *"You are aware of the fact that all who are in Asia turned away from me, among whom are Phygelus and Hermogenes. The Lord grant mercy to the house of Onesiphorus, for he often refreshed me and was not ashamed of my chains"* (2 Timothy 1:15–16 NASB). Disloyal people rejoice with you in good times, but flee from your bad times. Sons remain faithful through thick and thin. Do you have the heart of a son?

Prayer

Lord Jesus, I pray for the heart of a son. Amen

Application

What will you need to do today in order to remain loyal to your spiritual father and to the ministry you are currently serving under?

Hearing the voice of God

_____

_____

_____

_____

_____

_____

_____

_____

_____

Bible in a year
2 Chronicles 34 - 2 Chronicles 36

Disparaging Leaders

KEY VERSE

"The field is the world, the good seeds are the sons of the kingdom, but the tares are the sons of the wicked one"
(Matthew 13:38, NKJV)

Another mark of disloyalty is disparaging leaders. Miriam and Aaron got together to criticize Moses behind his back because he had married an Ethiopian woman. Moses did not hear, but the Bible states, *"The Lord heard"* (Numbers 12:1–2, NASB). So he came down and rebuked them before the Tabernacle. When the presence of the Lord left, Miriam was struck with leprosy that lasted seven days (Numbers 12:12-15, NASB).

One time I was receiving an offering for the church's construction. A man who did not know me from Adam started to criticize me in his home. While he was doing so, he became mute. He remained mute for a good six hours until people came and prayed with him. I did not hear, but the Lord heard and reacted. Disloyal servants disparage leaders behind their back; sons honor them. Which one are you?

Prayer

Father God, for as long as I serve in your kingdom, please allow me to leave a legacy of loyalty. In Christ's name, I pray. Amen.

Application

What are some good qualities you see in your spiritual father that you will begin to commend him for and talk to others about?

Hearing the voice of God

_____

_____

_____

_____

_____

_____

_____

_____

_____

_____

Bible in a year
Esdras 1 – Esdras 2

Power of Loyalty

KEY VERSE

"The field is the world, the good seeds are the sons of the kingdom, but the tares are the sons of the wicked one"
(Matthew 13:38, NKJV)

We have seen the nature of loyalty and the marks of disloyalty. Now let us look at the benefits of loyalty. David did not have the best soldiers in his army. Most of the people around him were people rejected by society. (1 Sam. 22: 1-2) Yet, with that ill-trained and ill-equipped army, he was able to kill the giants of Israel. The question is, what was the secret? The secret is found in 1 Chronicles 12:38. The Bible states, *"All these men of war, that could keep rank, came with a perfect heart to Hebron, to make David king"* (1 Chronicles 12:38).

Every time God wants to do great things, He raises a man or woman. However, a general can't do much without the loyalty of his soldiers. Are you loyal?

Prayer

Father God, there are so many things I can contribute to your kingdom; please allow loyalty to be one. I vow to be loyal in Jesus' mighty name. Amen.

Application

How are you planning to become a loyal soldier to your spiritual father and the great work the Lord has called him for?

Hearing the voice of God

_____

_____

_____

_____

_____

_____

_____

_____

_____

_____

Bible in a year
Esdras 3 – Esdras 6

May 23

Blessings of Loyalty

KEY VERSE
"The field is the world, the good seeds are the sons of the kingdom, but the tares are the sons of the wicked one"
(Matthew 13:38, NKJV)

Loyalty is a sacrifice, but yours will not be in vain. Talking about the giants, the Bible says, *"These were born to the giant in Gath, and they fell by the hand of David and by the <u>hand of his servants</u>"* (2 Chronicles 20:8). David had a giant-killing anointing over his life. His soldiers received the same. When you are loyal to a father, the grace that operates in his life flows into yours.

In sum, you must ask yourself: Am I operating with a son or a slave mentality? The slave is disloyal. He goes where the pastures are greener. The slave is attached to no one. He loves no one, has no sense of family; he is attached to himself, loves himself, and sees his interest. But a son sees the interests of his home. He is attached to his home. He rejoices when the house prospers because he knows it's his house. May you go from slavery to sonship in Jesus' name.

Prayer

I receive that word in Jesus' name. I proclaim that I am a son. Amen

Application

In what ways do you wish the ministry you are serving under would prosper, and how will you begin to contribute towards that prosperity?

Hearing the voice of God

_____

_____

_____

_____

_____

_____

_____

_____

_____

_____

Bible in a year
Esdras 7 – Esdras 10

May 24

Slavery Destroyed Our Sense of Submission

KEY VERSE

"The field is the world, the good seeds are the sons of the kingdom, but the tares are the sons of the wicked one"
(Matthew 13:38, NKJV)

One of the psychological consequences of slavery is the corruption of our sense of submission. The slave has a negative conception of authority. The master, the authority figure, whom he met when he came to the Americas was the one who enchained him, demeaned him, and made him work without ceasing. It was the person who whipped him. For the slave, the authority figure is a personification of evil. When a slave thinks of authority, he thinks of injustice, barbarism, and wickedness. It is no wonder that the slave is naturally rebellious. In his mind, the concept of a loving authority is an oxymoron. For him, a person in authority can never be loving because he had never seen the two mixed together. However, when we come to Christ, the slave mentality is replaced with a sonship mentality. We see God as both a sovereign king and a loving father. Thus, we pray, *"Our Father in heaven, hallowed be thy name. Thy kingdom comes"* (Matthew 6:10). What is your view of authority? What emotions do authority figures elicit in you when you see them?

Prayer

Heavenly Father, thank you for making sonship provisions for me in Christ my Lord and Savior. Amen.

Application

In what ways could you begin to celebrate the concept of authority? Why is this concept important to you?

Hearing the voice of God

_____

_____

_____

_____

_____

_____

_____

_____

_____

_____

Bible in a year
Nehemiah 1 – Nehemiah 3

May 25

Spiritual Slavery Also Destroyed Our Sense of Submission

KEY VERSE

"The field is the world, the good seeds are the sons of the kingdom, but the tares are the sons of the wicked one"

(Matthew 13:38, NKJV)

Natural slavery impacted some races, especially black people. Spiritual slavery affected the entire world. When Adam sinned against God, he triggered the law of rebellion. Hence, Paul writes, *"I find then a law, that evil is present with me, the one who wills to do good. For I delight in the law of God according to the inward man. But I see another law in my members, warring against the law of my mind, and bringing me into captivity to the law of sin which is in my members"* (Romans 7:21–23, NKJV). When man became a slave of sin, rebellion became natural to him. But when we become sons, we no longer war against God. He leads us. *"For as many as are led by the Spirit of God, these are sons of God"* (Romans 8:14, NKJV). Sons follow and obey. Do you have the heart of a son?

Prayer

Father God, I bless your name for the spiritual provisions I have in Christ Jesus. Amen.

Application

In what area of your Christian journey could you do a bit more following and obeying as you seek to become more loyal?

Hearing the voice of God

_____

_____

_____

_____

_____

_____

_____

_____

_____

Bible in a year
Nehemiah 4:1 – Nehemiah 7:3

What is Submission?

"The field is the world, the good seeds are the sons of the kingdom, but the tares are the sons of the wicked one"
(Matthew 13:38, NKJV)

Submission is to voluntarily bend our will to someone else's. It is not submission if you do something because you think it is a good idea or because you always wanted to do it. It is simply an opportunity. You know you are submissive when a person asks you to do something you do not want to do, but you do it anyway.

Now, submission is not inferiority. Just because you submit to someone does not mean that you are inferior. Apostle Paul said, *"You should think in the same way Christ Jesus does. In his very nature, he was God. But he did not think that <u>being equal with God</u> was something he should hold on to. Instead, he made himself nothing. He took on the very nature of a servant. He was made in human form. He appeared as a man. He came down to the lowest level. <u>He obeyed God completely</u>, even though it led to his death. He died on a cross"* (Philippians 2:5–8, NIRV). Jesus had the same nature as God the Father, yet He obeyed him. How do you feel when you have to submit to someone else?

Prayer

Father God, to be an effective son in your kingdom, submission is paramount. Help me to understand the value of submission. In Christ's name, I pray. Amen.

Application

What will submission in your own life begin to look like from here on out?

Hearing the voice of God

_____
_____
_____
_____
_____
_____
_____
_____
_____
_____
_____

Bible in a year
Nehemiah 7:4 – Nehemiah 8:18

May 27

Submission Comes from God

KEY VERSE

"The field is the world, the good seeds are the sons of the king-dom, but the tares are the sons of the wicked one"

(Matthew 13:38, NKJV)

Submission is a divine principle that flows out of God's nature. As Christians, we serve one God in three persons. The Father is the source of all things. The Bible says, *"For us, there is one God, the Father, of whom are all things, and we for Him; and one Lord Jesus Christ, through whom are all things, and through whom we live"* (1 Corinthians 8:6, NKJV). The Son submits to the Father. Thus, Jesus prayed at Gethsemane, *"Father, if it is Your will, take this cup away from Me; nevertheless, not My will, but Yours, be done"* (Luke 22:42, NKJV). And the Holy Spirit submits to the Son. Jesus says, "But when the Helper comes, whom I shall send to you from the Father, the Spirit of truth who proceeds from the Father, He will testify of Me" (John 15:26, NKJV). Notice that Jesus is the one who sends the Holy Spirit. Submission makes us look like God. Thus, whereas slaves rebel, people who carry a sonship mentality learn to submit. Ask God to help you to submit.

Prayer

Holy Spirit, I pray for a heart that submits. In Jesus' name, I pray. Amen.

Application

To whom could you practice the concept of submission today? Proceed with doing so, now!

Hearing the voice of God

_____

_____

_____

_____

_____

_____

_____

_____

_____

_____

Bible in a year
Nehemiah 9 – Nehemiah 11

May 28
God's Power Flows Through Submission

*"The field is the world, the good seeds are the sons of the king-
dom, but the tares are the sons of the wicked one"*
(Matthew 13:38, NKJV)

God's power and blessings flow through submission. Psalm
133 illustrates that very well. It says,

*"Behold, how good and how pleasant it is For brethren to dwell to-
gether in unity! It is like the precious <u>oil upon</u> the head, <u>Running down</u>
on the beard, The beard of Aaron, <u>Running down</u> on the edge of his
garments. It is like the dew of Hermon, <u>Descending upon</u> the moun-
tains of Zion; For there the LORD commanded the blessing— Life
forever"* (Psalm 133:1–3, NKJV).

The oil symbolizes God's power and the dew symbolizes
God's blessing. The oil flowed from Aaron's head to the rest
of the garment. The dew flowed from the top of the mountain to the surrounding region. The oil symbolizes power
and the dew blessing. God's power and blessings flow from
the top and everyone who is aligned partakes of them. Are
you submitted? Are you aligned?

Prayer

God, my King, in this season I pray to be aligned in your kingdom in order not to miss the oil and the dew flowing down from my spiritual parents. In Jesus Christ's name, I pray. Amen.

Application

What is causing or could cause you to become unaligned under your spiritual fathers covering, and what are you doing today to avoid that problem?

Hearing the voice of God

_____
_____
_____
_____
_____
_____
_____
_____
_____
_____

Bible in a year
Nehemiah 12 – Nehemiah 13

May 29
Rebellion comes from the Devil

KEY VERSE
"The field is the world, the good seeds are the sons of the kingdom, but the tares are the sons of the wicked one"
(Matthew 13:38, NKJV)

Submission comes from God, but Rebellion comes from the Devil. Isaiah describes the first act of sedition in the universe. He states, *"How you are fallen from heaven, O Lucifer, son of the morning! How you are cut down to the ground, You who weakened the nations"* (Isaiah 14:12, NKJV). The rebellion started when an angel called Lucifer decided to stand against God. The prophet continues, *"For you have said in your heart: 'I will ascend into heaven, I will exalt my throne above the stars of God; I will also sit on the mount of the congregation On the farthest sides of the north'"* (Isaiah 14:13, NKJV). Notice that the word "I" appears five times in the text, which means that pride is the root cause of rebellion. It becomes difficult to submit when we think we are better than others. The ego is the root of rebellion.

Prayer

In the powerful name of Jesus Christ, I command every seed of pride to be uprooted from the ground of my heart. Amen.

Application

FHow do you plan to deal with the challenges that are making it difficult for you to submit under the leadership of your spiritual covering?

Hearing the voice of God

_____

_____

_____

_____

_____

_____

_____

_____

_____

_____

Bible in a year
Esther 1 – Esther 4

May 30
Satan's power flows through rebellion

KEY VERSE

"The field is the world, the good seeds are the sons of the king-dom, but the tares are the sons of the wicked one"

(Matthew 13:38, NKJV)

If God's power flows through submission, Satan's power flows through <u>rebellion</u>. This is why in the Bible, it is viewed as witchcraft. Samuel asked Saul to kill living things that he found in the camp of the Amalekites. Saul spared king Agag and the best animals. When the prophet asked him why he did it, he said he was saving the animals for a sacrifice unto the Lord. The prophet responded, *"Rebellion is as the sin of witchcraft, And stubbornness is as iniquity and idolatry"* (1 Samuel 15:23, NKJV). <u>Rebellion</u> is equivalent to <u>witchcraft</u> and therefore, it exposes a person to demonic oppression and possession. Thus, Paul writes, *"And you, He made alive, who were dead in trespasses and sins, in which you once walked according to the course of this world, according to the prince of the power of the air, the spirit who now works in the sons of disobedience"* (Ephesians 2:1–2, NKJV). Notice that there is a spirit working through the sons of disobedience. And that spirit is identified as the "prince of the power of the air".

Prayer

I rebuke the spirit of rebellion and disobedience operating in my life. I replace them with the spirit of submission and obedience in Jesus Christ's name. Amen.

Application

In what ways could walking in obedience towards God and towards your spiritual father benefit you, and what plans will you have in place today to commit to that principle?

Hearing the voice of God

_____

_____

_____

_____

_____

_____

_____

_____

_____

_____

Bible in a year
Esther 5 – Esther 10

May 31

Refuse to Make Excuses

KEY VERSE
"The field is the world, the good seeds are the sons of the kingdom, but the tares are the sons of the wicked one"
(Matthew 13:38, NKJV)

To walk into your destiny as a son, you need to know how to walk in obedience. Here are some tips on how to walk in obedience. First, refuse to make excuses. Do not say, "The reason why I did not listen was..." Excuses will not change you. He who is good at making excuses, is not good at anything else. Refuse them. The Bible states, *"He who covers his sins will not prosper, But whoever confesses and forsakes them will have mercy"* (Proverbs 28:13, NKJV). Admit today that you tend to rebel against established authority and decide to live differently.

Secondly, decide to walk in obedience. The Bible states, *"He who covers his sins will not prosper,"* and the second part of the verse says, "But whoever confesses and forsakes them will have mercy" (Proverbs 28:13, NKJV). One of the greatest assets that God has given a man is the power to make decisions. He does not give it rocks, trees, or animals, but he has given it to men. You can change your destiny with one decision. Often God gives us grace after we have made up our minds. The Bible says concerning Daniel, he *"purposed in his heart that he would not defile"*. *"Now God had brought Daniel into the favor and goodwill of the chief of the eunuchs"* (Daniel 1:8-9, NKJV). If you decide to walk in submission, God will grant you grace.

Once you have decided to obey, stand strong on it. Tell your soul that it must submit. The Bible states, *"And from the days of John the Baptist until now the kingdom of heaven suffers violence, and the violent take it by force"* (Matthew 11:12, NKJV). When the Bible talks about being violent, it refers to an outward force that we exercise on others, but rather an inner pressure that we exact upon ourselves. Hence, the Bible says, *"He who is slow to anger is better than the mighty, And he who rules his spirit than he who takes a city"* (Proverbs 16:32, NKJV). To conquer your rebellion is better than taking over cities. Therefore, a son must be violent with himself.

Prayer

Lord of Host, train my hands for war against the flesh. In the mighty name of Christ, I pray. Amen.

Application

In what area(s) will you begin to be violent with yourself as a legitimate son of the kingdom? Begin today!

Hearing the voice of God

_____

_____

_____

_____

_____

_____

_____

_____

_____

_____

Bible in a year
Job 1 – Job 4

"The father receives the vision, but it is the sons who carry it out... Sons who follow the vision of a father are not in competition with each other. They complement each other"

Gregory Toussaint

June 1ˢᵗ

A Son Honors

KEY VERSE

"The field is the world, the good seeds are the sons of the kingdom, but the tares are the sons of the wicked one"

(Matthew 13:38, NKJV)

The first duty of a son towards his parents is honor. The Bible says, *"Honor your father and your mother, that your days may be long upon the land which the LORD your God is giving you"* (Exodus 20:12, NKJV). The Lord, speaking to post-exilic Jews, said, *"A son honors his father, And a servant his master. If then I am the Father, where is My honor?"* (Malachi 1:6, NKJV) What does it mean to honor? To honor means "to treat someone with great respect." Do you honor your biological and spiritual parents?

Prayer

Father God, train my heart to honor. In Jesus' name, I pray. Amen.

Application

How will you begin to cultivate a sense of honor towards your spiritual father?

Hearing the voice of God

_____

_____

_____

_____

_____

_____

_____

_____

_____

_____

Bible in a year
Job 5 – Job 7

June 2

A Son Honors in His Heart

KEY VERSE

"The field is the world, the good seeds are the sons of the kingdom, but the tares are the sons of the wicked one"

(Matthew 13:38, NKJV)

Honor is not simply an outward gesture; it is first an attitude of the heart. When honor does not proceed from the heart, it is hypocrisy. Therefore, Jesus said to the Pharisees, *"Well did Isaiah prophesy of you hypocrites, as it is these people honor Me with their lips, but their heart is far from Me"* (Mark 7:6, NKJV). Therefore, to know whether you honor your spiritual parents, all you must ask is, "What do you say in your heart about them?"

By the way, the thoughts of your heart are not as private as you think. The Bible says, *"Do not curse the king in your heart, even in your thoughts...For a bird of the air may carry your voice and a bird in flight may tell the matter"* (Ecclesiastes 10:20). In other words, when you have dishonor in your heart toward people, especially those in authority, they will know. The thoughts that you nurture in the deepest corners of your heart determine whether the honor exists or not. Ask the Holy Spirit to search your heart now.

Prayer

Holy Spirit of God, search my heart and expel hypocrisy from its dwelling. In Jesus' name. Amen.

Application

How will you begin to show genuine honor to your spiritual father without being hypocritical towards them? And what are some behaviors you will need to repent from?

Hearing the voice of God

_____

_____

_____

_____

_____

_____

_____

_____

_____

_____

Bible in a year
Job 8 – Job 11

June 3

A Son Honors with His Words

KEY VERSE

"The field is the world, the good seeds are the sons of the king-
dom, but the tares are the sons of the wicked one"

(Matthew 13:38, NKJV)

A son honors with his words. Honor begins in the heart
then is expressed through our words. The way you address
spiritual parents reveals whether you honor them or not.

One time I was talking to a friend, and he kept referring
to "Ti Boul" (Little Ball), but I could not understand who
he was referring to. So, I asked him who is "Ti Boul"? He
told me it was a pastor's nickname. Mind you, that pastor is
a pioneer in the Haitian Christian community in that area.
How do you refer to your spiritual father? Do you call him
"this guy"? All these habits speak a lot about how you view
him in your heart.

Furthermore, what you say about spiritual parents behind
his back also says a lot about whether you respect them or
not. Spiritual parents can and should be friendly. However,
we should never put them on the same level as a friend. They
are not not.

Prayer

Lord God, may the sentiments in my heart and the words from my lips honor my spiritual parents. In Jesus' name, I pray. Amen.

Application

How are you guarding yourself today from being too familiar with your spiritual father?

Hearing the voice of God

_____

_____

_____

_____

_____

_____

_____

_____

_____

_____

Bible in a year
Job 12 – Job 14

June 4
A Son Honors with His Actions

KEY VERSE

"The field is the world, the good seeds are the sons of the kingdom, but the tares are the sons of the wicked one"

(Matthew 13:38, NKJV)

You honor a father not only through words, but also through actions. One time, an assistant pastor was preaching the story of Jesus' triumphal entry into Jerusalem. To illustrate the message, he asked for the Senior Pastor to be on all four limbs to play the role of the donkey! Most people would not reach that level of disrespect. Be careful with little familiar actions like sitting on their chair without permission. Sometimes, the little things say a lot.

Prayer

Jesus, my Lord, in your name, I pray that my heart, my words, and my actions honor my spiritual father. Amen.

Application

How could you guard yourself from any signs of disrespect towards your spiritual father?

Hearing the voice of God

Bible in a year
Job 15 – Job 18

June 5
A Son Honors Through Giving

KEY VERSE
*"The field is the world, the good seeds are the sons of the king-
dom, but the tares are the sons of the wicked one"*
(Matthew 13:38, NKJV)

You also honor your spiritual parents through your giving.
The Word says, *"Let the elders who rule well be counted worthy
of double honor, especially those who labor in the word and doctrine.
The Scripture says, "You shall not muzzle an ox while it treads out
the grain," and, "The laborer is worthy of his wages"* (1 Timothy
5:17–18, NKJV). If you look at the context here, you see
that "honor" actually means "wages", in other words – money. Hence, sowing in the life of a parent is also a way to show
honor.

One time Saul had lost his donkey. After searching for three
days and three nights, someone told him that a prophet could
help. The first thing that Saul said to himself was, *"But look,
if we go, what shall we bring the man?"* (1 Samuel 9:7, NKJV) He
did not go to the prophet empty-handed. To him, sowing a
gift was a sign of honor.

Pat and I have made it a habit to honor the people that
God has placed in authority in our lives at the beginning of
each year. We honor our biological and spiritual parents at
the beginning of each year and ask them to pray for us. A lot
of blessings flow through them. Let honor be your portion
today!

Prayer

In this season Lord, I am learning about honor, help me to diligently apply what I've learned for the glory of Your name. Amen.

Application

What are you doing to ensure that the blessings of those whom God has placed in authority over your life will continue to flow?

Hearing the voice of God

_____

_____

_____

_____

_____

_____

_____

_____

_____

_____

Bible in a year
Job 19 – Job 21

June 6

A Son Imitates His Father

KEY VERSE

"The field is the world, the good seeds are the sons of the king-dom, but the tares are the sons of the wicked one"

(Matthew 13:38, NKJV)

A son not only honors, but also imitates. Unfortunately, imitation is extremely difficult for a person with a slave mentality. The reason is that the slave was forced to abandon his language, music, clothes, and religion. As a result, he has become defensive and indiscriminate about the little of the culture that he has left.

A slave dreads imitation, but to a son it comes naturally. The Bible encourages us to imitate both our Heavenly Father and spiritual fathers. As to Heavenly Father, it says, *"Be imitators of God as dear children"* (Ephesians 5:1, NKJV). As far as our spiritual fathers are concerned, it says, *"Imitate those who, through the faith and patience, inherit the promises"* (Hebrew 6:12). Thus, Paul says, *"For though you might have ten thousand instructors in Christ, yet you do not have many fathers; for, in Christ Jesus, I have begotten you through the gospel. Therefore I urge you, imitate me"* (1 Corinthians 4:15–16, NKJV). Why does God encourage us to imitate others? Because sometimes, it is easier to reproduce something when you have a flesh and blood example in front of you. May you learn well by watching and listening.

Prayer

Christ Lord, help me to be an effective imitator of my spiritual father. In Your name, I pray. Amen.

Application

What will you begin to do to appreciate the notion of imitation better?

Hearing the voice of God

_____

_____

_____

_____

_____

_____

_____

_____

_____

_____

Bible in a year
Job 22 – Job 24

A Son Imitates His Father's Character

KEY VERSE

"The field is the world, the good seeds are the sons of the kingdom, but the tares are the sons of the wicked one"
(Matthew 13:38, NKJV)

Paul says to the Corinthians, as a spiritual father, *"I urge you, imitate me"* (1 Corinthians 4:15–16, NKJV). So, what do we imitate in a spiritual parent? The first trait we must imitate is his character. Sometimes, people imitate a spiritual parent's mannerisms, walk, dresscode, and tone of voice but overlook his character. However, if you have missed the character, then you missed everything. It is the character that makes the man. You do not imitate every aspect of a spiritual father's character. Instead, you imitate the part of his character that reflects Christ. Therefore, Paul says, *"Imitate me, just as I also imitate Christ"* (1 Corinthians 11:1, NKJV). In other words, to the extent that I am imitating Christ, imitate me. Therefore, the author of Hebrews said, *"Imitate those who through faith and patience inherit the promises"* (Hebrews 6:12, NKJV). Faith and patience are characteristics found in Christ. Therefore, the author encourages the believers to imitate them. Before you imitate the traits of a father's life, you should ask whether they correspond with Christ. If they do, then you should imitate them. If they do not, then you should not.

Prayer

Holy Spirit of God, I pray for a discerning spirit to imitate from my spiritual father what is of Christ. In Christ's name, I pray. Amen.

Application

What is one trait you will set out today to imitate from your spiritual father, and how will that trait going to help you on becoming a better person?

Hearing the voice of God

_____

_____

_____

_____

_____

_____

_____

_____

_____

_____

Bible in a year
Job 25 – Job 28

June 8

A Son Imitates the Words of His Father

KEY VERSE

"The field is the world, the good seeds are the sons of the king-dom, but the tares are the sons of the wicked one"

(Matthew 13:38, NKJV)

A son imitates not only his father's character, but secondly his father's words. Jesus, as a model of a perfect son, said, *"For I have not spoken on My own authority; but the Father who sent Me gave Me a command, what I should say and what I should speak"* (John 12:49, NKJV). According to this verse, Jesus had developed two important habits. First, He paid attention to the words of His Father. Secondly, He spoke the words of His father. Are you hearing and speaking the words of your spiritual father?

Prayer

Christ my Lord, you have beautifully represented God the Father on earth, grant me wisdom so I may become a good representation of my spiritual father. In your name, I pray. Amen.

Application

What are some practices you've adopted or will begin to adopt that will help you with hearing and speaking the words of your spiritual father more often?

Hearing the voice of God

_____

_____

_____

_____

_____

_____

_____

_____

_____

Bible in a year
Job 29 – Job 31

June 9
A Son Imitates His Father's Actions

KEY VERSE
"The field is the world, the good seeds are the sons of the king-dom, but the tares are the sons of the wicked one"
(Matthew 13:38, NKJV)

A spiritual son imitates his father's character, words, and actions. Notice when Jesus says, *"Most assuredly, I say to you, the Son can do nothing of Himself, but what <u>He sees the Father</u> do; for whatever He does, the Son also <u>does in like manner</u>"* (John 5:19, NKJV). Jesus paid attention to what the Father was doing in heaven and imitated it. A spiritual son observes and imitates. One time, one of my spiritual sons said the Lord told him in prayer, "A student asks questions, but a son observes." This is true. Most of the things that a son learns in the house aren't learned by asking questions, but simply by observing. When your spiritual parents are ministering, on or off stage, take time to watch and learn.

Prayer
Father God, to effectively connect with my spiritual parents, I pray to become a smart observer and a wise imitator. In Jesus' name, I pray. Amen.

Application

What are some of the things you will begin to carry out today that you've observed from your spiritual father over the years?

Hearing the voice of God

_____

_____

_____

_____

_____

_____

_____

_____

_____

_____

Bible in a year
Job 32 – Job 34

June 10
If You Can Imitate, You Can Move Forward

KEY VERSE
"The field is the world, the good seeds are the sons of the king-dom, but the tares are the sons of the wicked one"
(Matthew 13:38, NKJV)

If you can imitate those ahead of you, you can move forward. Again, pay attention to the text, that *"Imitate those who through faith and patience inherit the promises"* (Hebrews 6:12, NKJV). We need to recognize that there are some people that God has placed in our lives who have already inherited at least part of their promises. They are walking in their Canaan and fulfilling their destiny. If we can imitate those people, we can also reach our potential. If you want to be the best at something, imitate the best. If you want to be a great basketball player, imitate Lebron James. Maybe Lebron won't be able to explain to you what he does, but you can emulate him by watching his every move. Imitation does not make us less intelligent or less anointed. It simply adds to the skills we already have.

Prayer
Father God, I pray for supernatural wisdom to see, through faith and patience, those who have fully or partially have inherited the promises. In the name of Christ my Lord, I pray. Amen.

Application

What are some skills you would like to imitate from your spiritual father and why?

Hearing the voice of God

_____
_____
_____
_____
_____
_____
_____
_____
_____
_____

Bible in a year
Job 35 – Job 37

June 11

The Power of Imitation

KEY VERSE
"The field is the world, the good seeds are the sons of the king-dom, but the tares are the sons of the wicked one"
(Matthew 13:38, NKJV)

I always give my testimony about my first sermons as a young preacher. One day I heard Pastor Eden McGuffie preaching, and I asked God to use me as He was using him. As I was about to leave the church, I heard an inner voice saying to buy the CDs of his sermons. I bought the CDs then spent the next two years listening to them every night, memorizing every verse. When I was invited somewhere to deliver a message, I would preach McGuffie's sermons, and people would acknowledge that I sounded just like my model. Today, I have my ministry and I am preaching around the world. But I started by imitating someone else. Imitation becomes a problem when it becomes servile. You can not limit yourself through imitation. You should use what you have received as a base, a foundation, to build upon and then add your own personal touch to it, making it yours. That honors your uniqueness, and you contribute to your progress. I am glad that I did. Are you imitating the positive things that you see in your spiritual family?

Prayer

Lord, I seek wisdom to imitate the good things that are in my spiritual family. In Jesus Christ's name, I pray. Amen.

Application

How much time and effort have you invested or will begin to invest in order to establish a foundation and a connection with your spiritual father?

Hearing the voice of God

_____

_____

_____

_____

_____

_____

_____

_____

_____

_____

Bible in a year
Job 38:1 – Job 40:2

June 12

Imitation Requires Humility

KEY VERSE
"The field is the world, the good seeds are the sons of the king-dom, but the tares are the sons of the wicked one"
(Matthew 13:38, NKJV)

The difficulty with imitation is that it requires humility. To imitate someone else, you must admit that the person is ahead of you or knows something you do not know. For some people, admitting this is a terrible blow to their ego. As a result, they would rather keep doing what they are doing, even though it is not taking them anywhere. This is pride and it simply needs to be crucified.

Prayer
Lord,I seek your strength and grace today to resist and expel pride out of my life. In Jesus' name, I pray. Amen.

Application

How could selflessness and humility help you through the process of imitating your spiritual father? What do you still feel needs to be crucified within yourself?

Hearing the voice of God

_____

_____

_____

_____

_____

_____

_____

_____

_____

Bible in a year
Job 40:3 – Job 42:17

What is a Vision

KEY VERSE

"The field is the world, the good seeds are the sons of the kingdom, but the tares are the sons of the wicked one"

(Matthew 13:38, NKJV)

A son carries a father's vision. A vision is a picture of the future that motivates our actions in the present. When God called Abraham, he promised him a land (Gen 12:1) and a seed (Gen 15:5). One day Abraham was discouraged. God gave him a clear picture of the future. The Bible states, "After these things, the word of the Lord came to Abraham in a vision, "He took him outside and said, *"Look up at the sky and count the stars—if indeed you can count them." Then he said to him, "So shall your descendants be"* (Genesis 15:1-5, NKJV).

One characteristic of a Godly vision is that it will appear crazy. God was talking to Abraham about having children like the stars of the heavens when he did not even have one child. The vision of a father can appear crazy, but God has a way of making them come to pass. Can you believe the crazy vision of your spiritual father?

Prayer

Father God, I pray for faith to believe what may appear to be crazy or impossible. In Jesus' name, I pray. Amen.

Application

Are you currently carrying your spiritual father's vision or your own? Why are you making the decision to forsake your own vision today?

Hearing the voice of God

_____

_____

_____

_____

_____

_____

_____

_____

_____

_____

Bible in a year
Psalms 1 – Psalms 9

A Vision Provides Direction

KEY VERSE

"The field is the world, the good seeds are the sons of the kingdom, but the tares are the sons of the wicked one"

(Matthew 13:38, NKJV)

When God called Abraham, He gave him a clear mandate. He needed to secure the land and be a channel for the promised seed, which would eventually become Jesus. So, God said to Abraham in the vision, *"I am the Lord, who brought you out of Ur of the Chaldeans, to give you this land to inherit it"* (Genesis 15:7, NKJV). The Lord also said in the same vision, *"Count the stars of the heavens, if you can…so shall your descendants be"* (Genesis 15:5, NKJV). The vision that God gave to Abraham became the guiding principle of Isaac, Jacob, Moses, the nation of Israel, and ultimately the church of Jesus Christ. Vision gives direction.

Imagine for a moment what would happen if each of your car's tires were moving in a different direction! How far do you think your car would get? Not very far, probably! Your car moves forward when you accelerate not simply because it has the engine that powers it but, also, because the transmission pushes all the tires in the same direction. Likewise, for a vision to move forward everyone must be headed in the same direction.

Prayer

Lord, I bless your name for the clear vision you have given my spiritual father. In Jesus' name, I pray. Amen.

Application

To what point has your own direction taken you? What are you doing now as a son to steer in the direction of your spiritual father's vision?

Hearing the voice of God

_____

_____

_____

_____

_____

_____

_____

_____

_____

Bible in a year
Psalms 10 – Psalms 17

June 15

A vision Produces Motivation

KEY VERSE

"The field is the world, the good seeds are the sons of the king-dom, but the tares are the sons of the wicked one"
(Matthew 13:38, NKJV)

When Abraham was discouraged about having a son, He said to God, *"Lord God, what will thou give me, seeing I go childless, and the steward of my house is this Eliezer of Damascus?"* (Genesis 15:2, NKJV) The Lord responded, *"This one shall not be your heir, but one who came from your own body shall be your heir"* (Genesis 15:4, NKJV). To encourage him, the Lord brought him outside and said, "He took him outside and said, *"Look up at the sky and count the stars—if indeed you can count them." Then he said to him, "So shall your descendants be"* (Genesis 15:5).

God motivated Abraham through a vision. The better you know the vision of the family, the more motivated you will be to serve in the house. As a son, you should take the time to read the house vision often and ask yourself "How can I help push it forward?"

Prayer

Holy Spirit, help me to see myself in my church vision. In Jesus Christ's name, I pray. Amen.

Application

How familiar are you with the vision of the congregation you are serving under, what are you currently doing to push that vision forward?

Hearing the voice of God

_____

_____

_____

_____

_____

_____

_____

_____

_____

_____

Bible in a year
Psalms 18 – Psalms 20

June 16

 ## *A vision Promotes Cooperation*

KEY VERSE

"The field is the world, the good seeds are the sons of the king-
dom, but the tares are the sons of the wicked one"
(Matthew 13:38, NKJV)

A common vision allows cooperation. The Bible states,
"Can two walk together unless they are agreed" (Amos 3:3, NKJV).
The father receives the vision, but it is the sons who execute
it. Since there is one vision, the sons will use their different
gifts and work together to make it happen. Sons who are
following a father's vision do not compete with each other.
They complement each other. Do you make it easy or difficult for people to work with you?

Prayer

Father God, as I engage to help drive my father's vision
forward, help me to be a team player, a collaborator and
an overall blessing to my spiritual family. In Christ's name I
pray. Amen.

Application

In what way will you begin to make a conscious effort to make it easier for others to work with you in your current ministry as you help push the vision forward?

Hearing the voice of God

_____

_____

_____

_____

_____

_____

_____

_____

_____

_____

Bible in a year
Psalms 21 – Psalms 25

June 17

A Vision Permits Evaluation

KEY VERSE

"The field is the world, the good seeds are the sons of the kingdom, but the tares are the sons of the wicked one"

(Matthew 13:38, NKJV)

The vision that God gave Abraham about the land and the seed later became the measuring rod by which the nation of Israel measured its success. When they did well, their land and their children would be blessed (Deut. 28:1-14). When they did evil, the opposite would occur (Deut. 18:15-19). The vision was supposed to be a measuring rod. Therefore, God was angry when Israel said, "We want a king like the other nations." They were supposed to measure their success based on Abraham's. A vision, not the customs of the nations. A son is successful when he is faithfully executing a father's vision. He does not judge his success by comparing himself with others.

Prayer

Father God, as I engage to help drive my father's vision forward, help me to be a team player, a collaborator and an overall blessing to my spiritual family. In Christ's name, I pray. Amen.

Application

To what extent are you currently executing the vision of your spiritual father, what could you do better to promote the vision?

Hearing the voice of God

_____

_____

_____

_____

_____

_____

_____

_____

_____

_____

Bible in a year
Psalms 26 – Psalms 31

June 18

Your Sonship will be Tested

KEY VERSE

*"The field is the world, the good seeds are the sons of the king-
dom, but the tares are the sons of the wicked one"*

(Matthew 13:38, NKJV)

After God the Father declared at Jesus' baptism, *"This is My
Son in whom I am well-pleased"* (Matthew 3:17). Jesus' sonship
was tested. Jesus was tested by both God (Matt. 4:11) and
Satan (Luke 4:1). However, the temptation in the wilderness
was not the only test that Jesus had to pass. The Bible says,
"He was tempted in all things" (Hebrews 4:15). A son is always
being tempted. Ask God to give you grace for the temptations you will face as a son.

Prayer

Lord, prepare me for trials. May your grace and mercy be
with me. In Jesus' name, I pray. Amen!

Application

What are some spiritual disciplines you are currently practicing today that will later equip you for the inevitable temptations you will likely face as a son?

Hearing the voice of God

_____

_____

_____

_____

_____

_____

_____

_____

_____

_____

Bible in a year
Psalms 32 – Psalms 35

A Son Succeeds

KEY VERSE

"The field is the world, the good seeds are the sons of the kingdom, but the tares are the sons of the wicked one"

(Matthew 13:38, NKJV)

A son succeeds. However, you cannot have success if you have not been tested. Thus, your sonship will be tested. Jesus' sonship was tested by both God (Matt. 4:1) and Satan (Luke. 4:1). Yours will be tested by both as well. The test will come through different people and circumstances, but it will happen nonetheless!

Prayer

Lord, prepare me for the tests. May your grace and mercy see me through. In Jesus' name, I pray. Amen.

Application

What are some spiritual principles are you currently applying or will begin to put in place lest you fold under the pressure of the temptations await?

Hearing the voice of God

_____
_____
_____
_____
_____
_____
_____
_____
_____
_____

Bible in a year
Psalms 36 – Psalms 39

Silence Test

KEY VERSE

"The field is the world, the good seeds are the sons of the king-dom, but the tares are the sons of the wicked one"
(Matthew 13:38, NKJV)

The first test you will face as a son is the silence test. This test is when the father is completely silent, as if he does not know you exist or has completely forgotten about you. The Father spoke to Joseph about Jesus when he was two years old. From then on, God was silent for 28 years. God then spoke, regarding Jesus again, when He was 30 years old in the waters of the Jordan (Matt. 3:17). Imagine how those years must've been during that time from a human perspective. Faithfulness, humility, and inner motives are tested. How do you react when you are working and a father is silent?

Prayer

Father God, condition my heart with patience and faith so I may overcome the silent test. In Christ the Lord, I pray. Amen.

Application

How are you currently handling the silent test? How is the vision propelling you to still move forward today?

Hearing the voice of God

_____

_____

_____

_____

_____

_____

_____

_____

_____

_____

Bible in a year
Psalms 40 – Psalms 44

June 21

Isolation Test

KEY VERSE

"The field is the world, the good seeds are the sons of the king-dom, but the tares are the sons of the wicked one"
(Matthew 13:38, NKJV)

The second test that a son goes through is the isolation test. This is the time when you are relocated to a place where it seems like nothing is happening. That was the case for Jesus for twenty-eight years when he was assigned to Nazareth. No one wants to be in there because *"Nothing good comes from Nazareth"* (John 1:46). You are in Nazareth when it seems like nothing good is happening in your life. You are in Nazareth when your friends have moved to another church or have branched out independently. You seem to be the only one left. It seems that nothing good is happening. In Nazareth, you must decide whether to follow others or stick to God's process.

Prayer

Father God, when I'm in Nazareth, help me to keep my eyes on you and you alone. In Jesus' mighty name, I pray. Amen.

Application

How are you mustering the inner strength to still remain in Nazareth and completely forsake your spiritual father's vision despite the temptations to surrender and retreat?

Hearing the voice of God

_____

_____

_____

_____

_____

_____

_____

_____

_____

Bible in a year
Psalms 45 – Psalms 50

June 22

Recognition Test

KEY VERSE

"The field is the world, the good seeds are the sons of the king-dom, but the tares are the sons of the wicked one"
(Matthew 13:38, NKJV)

After serving in Nazareth for 30 years, God declared to the nations, *"This is my Son in Whom I am well-pleased"* (Matthew 3:17, NKJV). As soon as those words were said, Satan threw three of his worst blows His way. When a father praises you publicly, you need to remain humble and, most important-ly, in prayer because the devil will try to prove the father wrong. When your father praises you, be encouraged but not over-confident or cocky. Pray instead!

Prayer

Father God, equip me for the recognition test. Allow me to be matured and anchored in You. In Christ's name, I pray. Amen.

Application

How do you plan to handle the praises and the accolades of your spiritual father and still ascribe to the Lord of glory?

Hearing the voice of God

_____

_____

_____

_____

_____

_____

_____

_____

_____

_____

Bible in a year
Psalms 51 – Psalms 56

Food Test

KEY VERSE

"The field is the world, the good seeds are the sons of the kingdom, but the tares are the sons of the wicked one"

(Matthew 13:38, NKJV)

The fourth test is the food test. That test happens when you have needs and are in a position in the ministry to serve yourself. What do you do? Satan administered the food test to Jesus when he said, *"If You are the Son of God, command this stone to <u>become bread</u>"* (Luke 4:3, NKJV). Satan gives you the food test when he shows all your needs and how you can serve your needs with the resources God has entrusted to you. Basically, the food test is the temptation to become a thief.

Prayer

Father God, you have supplied all my needs according to your riches and glory. Thank you for allowing me to be a good steward of your resources. In Jesus' name, I pray. Amen.

Application

Pray and ask God for grace to remain steadfast in your values, character, and convictions so you may prevail over the food test.

Hearing the voice of God

_____

_____

_____

_____

_____

_____

_____

_____

_____

_____

Bible in a year
Psalms 57 – Psalms 62

Power Test

KEY VERSE

"The field is the world, the good seeds are the sons of the kingdom, but the tares are the sons of the wicked one"
(Matthew 13:38, NKJV)

The fifth test is the power test. Satan set him on top of the temple and said, "If You are the Son of God, throw Yourself down from here For it is written: *"He shall give His angels charge over you, To keep you,' and, "In their hands, they shall bear you up, Lest you dash your foot against a stone"* (Luke 4:9–11, NKJV). Satan was asking Jesus to mobilize the angels of heaven without the Father's authorization. He was trying to elicit in him a thirst for power, a thirst to take control. Sons fall into that temptation when they get to the point that they start making their own decision independent of their father's will.

Prayer

Father God, protect my heart so I may not be trapped in the fowler's snare. In Christ mighty name, I pray. Amen.

Application

In what area(s) of your life do you still value your spiritual father's advice? Pray and ask God for the grace to remain a son who is dependent on their spiritual father.

Hearing the voice of God

_____

_____

_____

_____

_____

_____

_____

_____

_____

Bible in a year
Psalms 63 – Psalms 68

June 25

Glory Test

KEY VERSE

"The field is the world, the good seeds are the sons of the king-dom, but the tares are the sons of the wicked one"
(Matthew 13:38, NKJV)

The sixth test is the glory test. Satan said to Jesus, *"And the devil said to Him, All this authority I will give You, and their glory; for this has been delivered to me, and I give it to whomever I wish"* (Luke 4:6, NKJV). As a son, you often get the glory test when you start becoming popular and people are talking well about you. You begin to get puffed up. You feel like there is nothing that the father is doing that you cannot do.

Prayer

Lord, God Almighty, all glory, honor and praise belong to You and to You alone. In Christ' name, I pray. Amen.

Application

How do you handle praises in your current ministry depart-
ment, and do you seek to always give God the glory?

Hearing the voice of God

_____

_____

_____

_____

_____

_____

_____

_____

_____

_____

Bible in a year
Psalms 69 – Psalms 72

June 26

The Responsibility Test

KEY VERSE

*"The field is the world, the good seeds are the sons of the king-
dom, but the tares are the sons of the wicked one"*
(Matthew 13:38, NKJV)

The seventh test is the responsibility test. Jesus faced that test in the Garden of Gethsemane. When he looked at the cup of suffering, something inside Him told Him that it was too much. But after He prayed, *"If it is your will, take this cup away from me,"* He said, *"Nevertheless not My will but Yours be done" (Luke 22:42, NKJV).* You are given the responsibility test when you feel like it is not humanly possible to do the task you have been given. That's when you need to remember his strength is made perfect in our weaknesses (2 Corinthians 12:7-10). Ask God to strengthen you.

Prayer

God, your strength is made perfect in my weaknesses. Strengthen me today for the responsibility now and those ahead. In Your Son, Jesus Christ' name, I pray. Amen.

Application

How do you plan to become more loyal and committed to the ministry the Lord has entrusted you?

Hearing the voice of God

_____

_____

_____

_____

_____

_____

_____

_____

_____

_____

Bible in a year
Psalms 73 – Psalms 76

The Demotion Test

KEY VERSE

"The field is the world, the good seeds are the sons of the kingdom, but the tares are the sons of the wicked one"
(Matthew 13:38, NKJV)

The last and perhaps most challenging test for a son is the demotion test. Jesus as a son, went through many levels of demotion. First, He was demoted from God to man (Phil. 2:5-7). Now, as a man, He was demoted farther to dying on the cross. The execution sentence is reserved for the lowest criminal (Phil. 2:8). Finally, because He agreed to that demotion, He was raised to a place even higher than He was before (Phil 2:10). Many sons quit when they are demoted. As a result, they miss their best season! What is your reaction when you are demoted?

Prayer

Father God, on top of the mountain you are my strength and in the valley you are my strength. Guide me so I may stick to Your plan, for all my resources are in You. In Jesus name, I pray. Amen.

Application

How do you prepare yourself to still guard your heart and remain consistent if and when given a lesser role in the overall vision of your spiritual father?

Hearing the voice of God

_____

_____

_____

_____

_____

_____

_____

_____

_____

Bible in a year
Psalms 77 – Psalms 78

A Son is Protected

KEY VERSE

"The field is the world, the good seeds are the sons of the king-dom, but the tares are the sons of the wicked one"
(Matthew 13:38, NKJV)

One of the first and most important rewards of a son is protection. The Bible tells of the story of Joshua, who went to war with Amalekites. Moses, his spiritual father, was on the mountain praying. The Bible relates, *"And so it was, when Moses held up his hand, that Israel prevailed; and when he let down his hand, Amalek prevailed"* (Exodus 17:11, NKJV). In other words, Joshua and his army became victorious because of a father's intercession on the mountain. Without Moses on the mountain, Israel would have lost the war; and Joshua, most likely, would have died. Having a spiritual covering brings protection over your life.

Prayer

Father God, thank you for the Moses you have placed in my life. I abide under the shadow of the Almighty. In Jesus Christ's name, I pray. Amen.

Application

What is your responsibility as a son to ensure you are re-
maining under the covering of your spiritual father?

Hearing the voice of God

_____

_____

_____

_____

_____

_____

_____

_____

_____

_____

Bible in a year
Psalms 79 – Psalms 83

June 28

A Son is Anointed

KEY VERSE

"The field is the world, the good seeds are the sons of the kingdom, but the tares are the sons of the wicked one"
(Matthew 13:38, NKJV)

The second blessing is anointing. As we had studied in the previous volume, a son is connected to a generational anointing. Describing the generational anointing flowed from Aaron and his spiritual descendants, David says *"Behold, how good and how pleasant it is For brethren to dwell together in unity! It is like the precious oil upon the head, Running down on the beard, The beard of Aaron, Running down on the edge of his garments"* (Psalm 133:1–2, NKJV). The oil which represents generational anointing flows through alignment. Are you aligned with the father of the house?

Prayer

Father God, thank you for the blessings flowing through my spiritual parents at Tabernacle of Glory. I am aligned and I am anointed. In Jesus Christ's name, I pray. Amen.

Application

How can you better align yourself today to partake in the anointing that is over your spiritual father?

Hearing the voice of God

_____

_____

_____

_____

_____

_____

_____

_____

_____

_____

Bible in a year
Psalms 84 – Psalms 88

June 30

A Son is Blessed

KEY VERSE

"The field is the world, the good seeds are the sons of the king-dom, but the tares are the sons of the wicked one"
(Matthew 13:38, NKJV)

Third, a son is blessed. A blessing has many components. First, it is a force from God that causes God's creation to fulfill its created purpose. For example, after God had created Adam and Eve, the Bible states, *"And God blessed them, saying, 'Be fruitful and multiply, and fill the waters in the seas, and let birds multiply on the earth"* (Genesis 1:22, NKJV). God had already put the capacity in them to multiply, but the blessing will cause it to manifest. When you are blessed, you flourish. Second, a blessing has an outward component. When Jacob was blessing His children, he said, *"The Angel who has redeemed me from all evil, Bless the lads; Let my name be named upon them, And the name of my fathers Abraham and Isaac; And let them grow into a multitude amid the earth"* (Genesis 48:16, NKJV). When you are blessed, you have angelic help to fulfill your purposes. All privileges are extended to a son. May the Lord Help you to be a true son.

Prayer

Lord, thank you for all your blessings. Help me to live out the character of a true son. In Jesus Christ's name, I pray. Amen.

Application

What are some practices will you begin to carry out everyday to ensure you are being a good son to your spiritual father?

Hearing the voice of God

_____
_____
_____
_____
_____
_____
_____
_____
_____
_____

Bible in a year
Psalms 89 – Psalms 91

Afterword

"The Lord bless you
and keep you;
the Lord make his face shine on you
and be gracious to you;
the Lord turn his face toward you
and give you peace."
(Numbers 6:24-25, NIV)

Biography

Gregory Toussaint (B.S., LL.M., Th.M., D.E.A) is the Senior Pastor of Tabernacle of Glory in Miami. Home to more than 12 campuses in different cities worldwide, Pastor Greg is a gifted teacher who preaches weekly in 4 languages, Kreyol, English, French, and Spanish. He is also a prolific writer who has written more than 30 books. Some of those titles are Fruits of the Holy Spirit, Jezebel Unveiled, Thy Kingdom Come, 10 of which are Amazon Best-sellers. Pastor Greg is also an Evangelist who organizes large-scale conferences and crusades in different parts of the world. He moves strongly in the supernatural, especially in healing, deliverance, and the prophetic. Pastor Greg is involved in Humanitarian work in Haiti, the Dominican Republic, and Ghana. Pastor Greg holds degrees in Business, Law, and Theology. He is married to Patricia Toussaint and has two children. His goal in life is to show forth the glory of God wherever he goes.

Testimonies

If this book has impacted your life,
please share your testimony with us.
Pastor G Library

Email:
pastorgslibrary@gmail.com

Mailing Address
990 NE 125th Street Suite 200
North Miami, FL 33161

If you happen to be in the Miami area on a Weekend, please visit us.

Tabernacle of Glory
Email:contact@tabernacleofglory.net
Website: www.tabernacleofglory.net
990 NE 125th Street, Suite 200
North Miami, FL 33161
(305) 899-0101

Made in United States
Orlando, FL
30 March 2022

16323899R00120